MW00861033

SAM CHOY'S
IN THE KITCHEN
FAMILY RECIPES
featured on
khon2

PRESENTING SPONSORS

Spectrum

ASSOCIATE SPONSORS

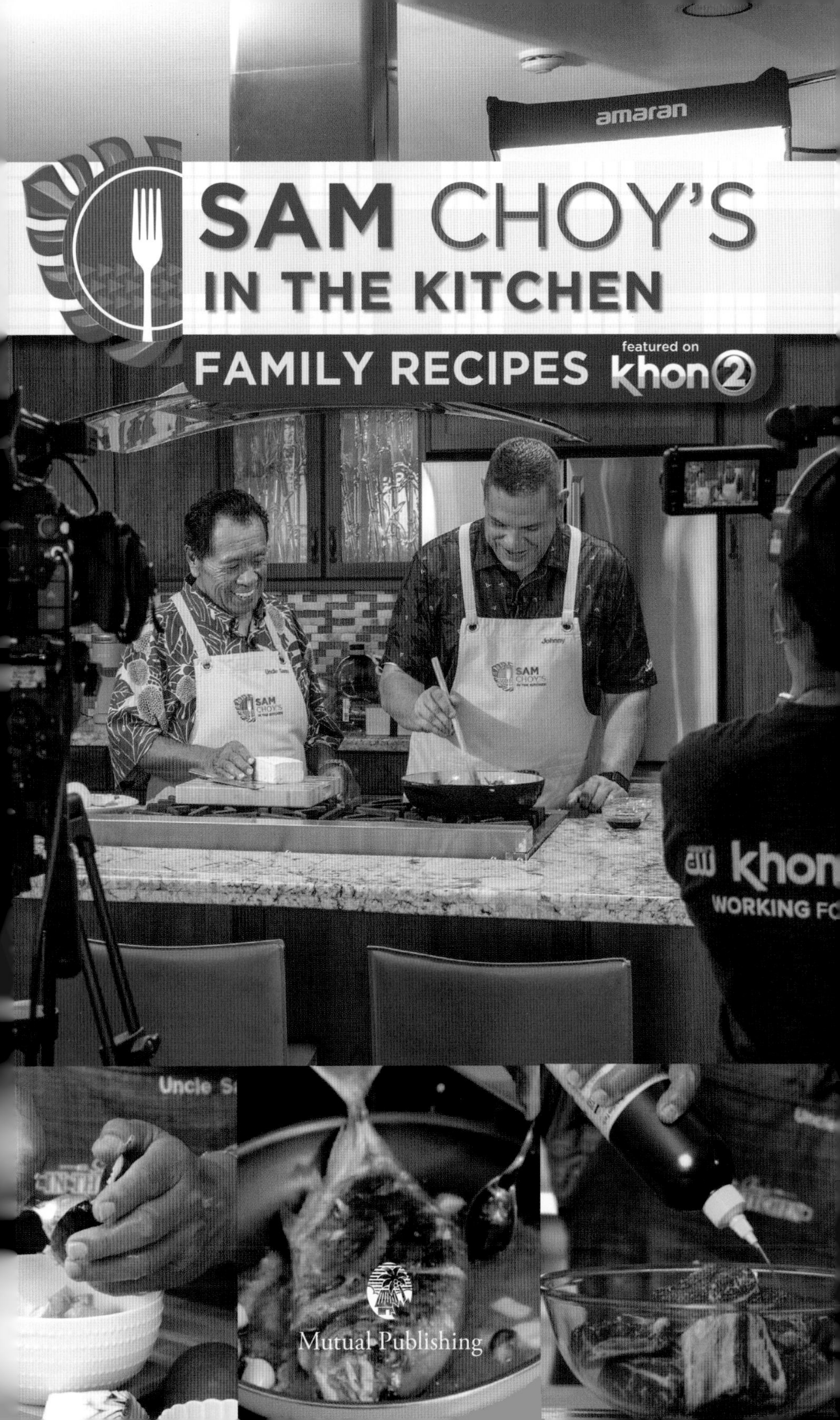
amaran
SAM CHOY'S
IN THE KITCHEN
FAMILY RECIPES
featured on
khon2
Johnny
khon
WORKING FO
Uncle S
Mutual Publishing

ISBN: 978-1-949307-65-8
Library of Congress Control Number: 2024941733

Layout and design by Jane Gillespie
All photos © KHON2 except photos on pages: iii (top), x (top), xi (top), 11, 12, 18, 24, 25, 100, 101, 152, 153, front cover © Douglas Peebles
First Printing, October 2024

Mutual Publishing, LLC
1215 Center Street, Suite 210
Honolulu, Hawaiʻi 96816
Ph: 808-732-1709 / Fax: 808-734-4094
email: info@mutualpublishing.com
www.mutualpublishing.com

Printed in South Korea

CONTENTS

SIDES • 43

MAIN DISHES • 61

BEEF AND PORK

POULTRY

SEAFOOD

FOREWORD

KHON2 is dedicated to airing programming and content which reflects the interests and the culture of the people of Hawai'i. In 2015, we put out a challenge to our staff to help us come up with a new local program to air on Sundays at 6:30 p.m. The entire station got involved with collaborating and coming up with different ideas for this new show. We wanted to use this popular family/dinner hour to create something unique, special, and a destination program to give Hawai'i families a fun way to end their weekend and prepare for the week ahead.

We brainstormed several different options, but when we met award-winning Hawai'i chef, author, restaurateur, founding contributor of Pacific Rim Cuisine, and "God Father of Poke" Chef Sam Choy, we knew immediately that we wanted to work with him! Soon thereafter, we created an exciting partnership and eventually launched *Sam Choy's in the Kitchen*, on Sunday night on KHON2 with an encore presentation on KHII.

Our original concept was about sustainability and how we could encourage viewers to create delicious meals from food they already had in their pantry and refrigerators. Chef Sam inspired people to utilize their leftovers in new and creative ways. He helped people see how they can take their boring leftovers and turn them into an even more extraordinary meal. Chef Sam shared his family recipes and his helpful tips to make cooking easier in the kitchen. We

added KHON2 Lifestyle Host John Veneri as Sam's co-host and "stew chef" to assist in the kitchen and to ask Chef Sam the questions we all wanted to know to learn about cooking, grilling, flavor profiles, and plating our dishes. We are so excited to entertain Hawai'i viewers every week with inspiring recipes and entertaining guests—Sam and John together make cooking fun for everyone!

Now in our ninth season, we are proud to have produced over 200 episodes featuring Hawai'i families who love to cook and others who just love to eat! Friends and celebrity guests like Frank DeLima, Hawai'i's Governor Josh Green, Kai Lenny, Chef Aarón Sánchez, Jake Shimabukuro, Kelly Slater, Tumua Tuinei, Max Unger, and many more have joined our culinary duo—and welcomed us into their homes, sharing their special recipes. Sam has used his culinary magic to create memorable dishes along with many amazing local families who graciously invited us into their kitchens and let Chef Sam and our production crew rifle through their pantry and fridges.

On behalf of KHON2, we want to say mahalo to the many sponsors throughout the years who have supported us and championed the show, including Ala Moana Hotel, Aloha Shoyu, Clos Du Bois, D. Otani Produce, Halm's Enterprises, Hawai'i Financial Federal Credit Union, Kaua'i Shrimp, National Kidney Foundation, Non-Stop Travel, Spectrum, Subway Hawai'i, Sun Noodle, and many more. Also, I would like to recognize our amazing *Sam Choy's in the Kitchen* Crew (past and present), who have dedicated countless hours to this program, led by Jennifer Salviejo, John Veneri, Alex Garcia, Reiss Kaneshiro, Taylon Nieto, Daisy Mae Tiposo, Kevin Luke, Pamela Young, Tyann Clark, Jesse Macadangdang, Kerry Yoshida, Richard Gonzalez, Kawehi Thoene, Lynette Martin, and the entire KHON2 team who pour their heart and soul into each episode.

This cookbook is a testament to the creativity and culinary skills of world-renowned Chef Sam Choy and to the people of Hawai'i who love the mixed plates we share and enjoy where all our culture and cuisines come together to complement each other. We hope you will love every recipe and that this cookbook will inspire all home cooks who stand in front of an open refrigerator every night wondering what the heck to make for dinner. Chef Sam turns that frustration into excitement showing you how easy and quick it is to whip up a delicious, wholesome meal that won't break the bank and can be made without an additional trip to the store.

We are so pleased to present *Sam Choy's in the Kitchen Family Recipes* for you and your 'ohana to share. Enjoy your time in the kitchen and with each other, because as Chef Sam says, "When Sam Choy's in the kitchen, you can do the cooking."

— Kristina Lockwood,
KHON2 Vice President and General Manager

INTRODUCTION

Cooking is a family affair. I learned how to cook and started to love cooking at home with my family, watching and learning from my mom, Clairemoana, and my dad, Hung Sam. Their influences form the basis of everything I do today and reflects much of what I believe in. I have so many wonderful memories of spending time in our family kitchen making meals. My parents were so good at using whatever was in the fridge or pantry. They planned ahead, sure, but they also knew how to be creative and improvise with leftovers, mixing and matching ingredients, and not letting food go to waste.

In 2015 I had the crazy idea of visiting family kitchens across Hawai'i—partly because I was curious to see what they had in their refrigerators and pantries, and also to teach people how to cook delicious meals using what they had on hand. These days, people in the islands are so much more aware of the threat of food insecurity and the importance of food sustainability. I think people are realizing that our single-use and throw away mentality isn't doing anything good for the planet, for our pocketbooks, and for our families. At the same time, we are all so busy. Time constraints and economic pressure pushes us into cooking ruts—it's no wonder families get sick of the same old leftovers and the same old dishes.

So I started visiting families who graciously invited me into their kitchens, and I found that people had plenty to work with. They just needed the encouragement and guidance to reinvent and improvise recipes and to take leftovers, stretch them out, and turn them into a whole new meal.

Luckily, we got the attention of KHON2 and with their help, *Sam Choy's in the Kitchen* became a television show which opened up a whole new audience to us and some amazing, generous families who were willing to share their kitchen with us. It's been a blast.

This cookbook is the culmination of our nine seasons. We wanted to share with you some of the recipes we created in these amazing family kitchens across Hawai'i. Some of them may seem real simple, and that's the point. These recipes are meant to inspire you and give you permission and guidance to reimagine that container of leftovers and turn them into something new. Got leftover donuts but want to do something new with them? Make a bread pudding! Have just a little stew leftover but need to feed a family of four? Stretch it out by adding some veggies and make stew sliders. You don't have to break the bank or make yet another trip to the grocery store to create something tasty with your leftovers. And there are so many amazing locally-made products available—sauces, seasonings, dressings—that you can keep in your pantry to elevate flavor profiles or alter them.

Here in Hawai'i, we are known for creating mixed-up plates of various cuisines that complement each other. These family recipes are meant to inspire all home cooks and bring excitement back into the kitchen. Next time you find yourself standing in front of an open refrigerator, instead of feeling frustrated, you'll feel creative and will have the confidence to grab some of this and some of that and create something delicious and new for your family that celebrates the flavors of Hawai'i.

— Chef Sam Choy

PŪPŪ

Blackened ‘Ahi Sashimi

Serves 4

Rub
¼ teaspoon cayenne pepper
1 teaspoon garlic salt
1 teaspoon paprika
½ teaspoon black pepper

1 pound fresh ‘ahi, cut into small rectangular blocks

Mix rub ingredients together in a small bowl.

Dust ‘ahi pieces with dry rub mixture. In a pan over high heat, sear each side for about 30 seconds. Remove fish from hot pan, place in a smaller dish and put in the freezer for 5 minutes to stop the cooking process. Slice and serve on mixed greens.

Here’s a delicious pūpū you can make super fast. Sear the ‘ahi really quick after seasoning. And here’s the trick to stop the cooking—after searing, put it in the freezer for a few minutes. You know, I always tell people, tuna is expensive. If you overcook tuna, you would’ve been better off buying it in the can.

Chinese-Style Sashimi

Serves 2 to 4

2 cups shredded local cabbage
1 pound fresh local 'ahi
2 tablespoons minced ginger
½ cup minced cilantro
½ cup peanut oil
3 tablespoons Aloha Shoyu Soy Sauce

Lay a bed of shredded cabbage on a pūpū platter. Cut the 'ahi into even slices. Garnish with ginger and cilantro.

Heat peanut oil until very hot. Pour soy sauce over 'ahi and sear with hot peanut oil.

Fast and easy. It all starts with some freshly caught fish. Make sure the oil is smoking hot. Fun to make and even better to eat.

MICHAEL AND KEHAU KAUAKAHI

I bet you never thought of putting a Portuguese sausage seasoning on ‘ahi. But try it. The flavor is wow. But remember, you don’t need to have a large spice collection to season ‘ahi sashimi. Sometimes simple is best: just some salt, maybe paprika. You don’t need a lot.

Seared Sashimi

Serves 2 to 4

1 packet NOH Foods Hawaiian Style Portuguese Sausage Seasoning Mix
½ teaspoon garlic salt
Salt and pepper, to taste
2 large fillets fresh ‘ahi
1 cup diced cabbage

In a small bowl, create a dry rub by combining the seasoning mix, garlic salt, salt, and pepper. Coat fish fillets on all sides with the dry rub mixture.

Sear fish on high heat for 1 to 2 minutes on each side. Remove fish from heat and place in the freezer for 3 to 4 minutes to stop the cooking process. Remove from freezer, slice into sashimi size pieces, and serve on a bed of diced cabbage.

Firecracker Fish Roll

Serves 4

1 pound fresh ‘ahi
1 pound fresh salmon
½ teaspoon wasabi
½ cup mayonnaise
1 teaspoon sesame oil
2 tablespoons Aloha Shoyu Spicy Da Yaki Sauce
8 nori sheets
2 cups cooked rice
1 tablespoon oil
½ teaspoon unagi sauce

Slice ‘ahi and salmon into long pieces. Add wasabi, toss together lightly, and set aside.

In a small bowl, add mayonnaise, sesame oil, and yaki sauce; mix until well-combined.

On each sheet of nori, spread an even layer of rice and add pieces of fish. Wrap tightly and fry in hot oil until the nori is crispy. Drizzle with spicy mayonnaise mixture and unagi sauce.

We visited Chef James Martin of Da Bald Guy food truck on the North Shore of O‘ahu, who competed on the sixteenth season of The Great Food Truck Race in 2023, and made these firecracker fish rolls. You aren’t actually cooking the fish. What you want to do is sear the outside of the nori until it’s crispy and inside, the fish will be medium-rare.

Ono Poke Dome

Serves 4

1 pound fresh ono, cut into small cubes
½ small red onion, finely diced
½ cup chopped taegu
1 tablespoon sesame oil
2 tablespoons Aloha Shoyu Soy Sauce
2 tablespoons chopped green onions
1 avocado, diced
1 tomato, diced
2 tablespoons kalbi marinade

Garnish
Cilantro sprigs

In a bowl, add ono, onions, taegu, sesame oil, soy sauce, and green onions. Mix well.

In a separate bowl, add avocado, tomatoes, and kalbi marinade. Mix well.

Spoon ono poke into a serving bowl. Top with avocado mixture and garnish with cilantro.

Out in Kona on the Big Island where I live, you can see the charter boats out in the mornings when the ono are running. Ono, or wahoo, is a sustainable Hawaiian fish that has a mild, sweet flavor. It's a good fish, especially for poke. It's a lean fish so if you cook it too long, it gets dry so you have to be careful.

KULANI AND FRED WATSON

Spicy Salmon Poke Nori Cups

Serves 4

½ pound fresh salmon, cut into 1-inch cubes
½ yellow onion, sliced
½ cup sliced green onions
3 to 4 packages nori squares
2 tablespoons Aloha Shoyu Poke Sauce
2 tablespoons mayonnaise
Sriracha

Sushi Rice
2 cups cooked white rice
1½ tablespoons rice vinegar
1½ tablespoons sugar
Salt, to taste

Garnish
Sriracha, to taste
¼ cup sliced green onions

Preheat oven to 400°F. In a mixing bowl, combine the salmon, yellow onions, and green onions. Set aside.

To make the Sushi Rice, in another bowl, combine rice, rice vinegar, sugar, and salt. Mix well. Place nori squares in a muffin pan. With wet hands, make rice balls to fit into each nori cup.

To the salmon bowl, add poke sauce and mayonnaise and mix well. Spoon salmon mixture on top of each rice ball. Bake for 10 to 15 minutes. Garnish with sriracha and remaining green onions.

We call mayonnaise cowboy gravy. It's the most important condiment. My sister was married to a guy from Waimea and all those guys at the lūʻau, they all had a bottle of mayonnaise in their back pocket. They'd be putting it on everything, the lau lau, hot rice, everything. That's why we started calling it cowboy gravy.

‘Ahi Poke with Cucumbers and Tomatoes

Serves 4

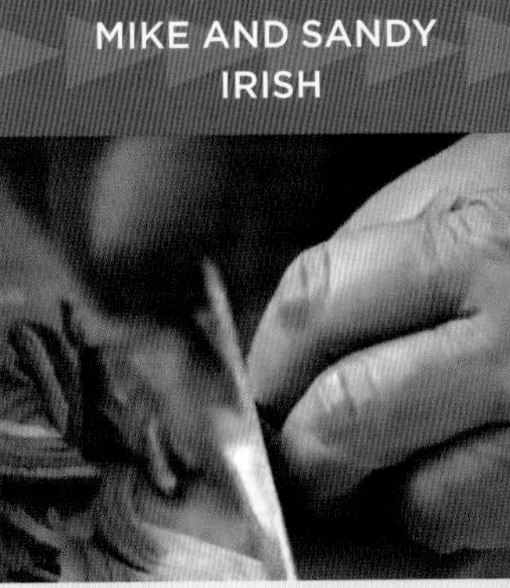

3½ pounds fresh ‘ahi, cubed
½ teaspoon Hawaiian salt
½ medium red onion, sliced
1 cucumber, quartered and chopped
10 cherry tomatoes, quartered
1 tablespoon chojang sauce
2 tablespoons Ohana Flavors Shoyu Poke Sauce
4 tablespoons Halm’s Kim Chee Poke Sauce

In a large bowl, season the ‘ahi with Hawaiian salt. Combine ‘ahi with remaining ingredients. Toss lightly and serve.

I like to season the fish first with just a little bit of Hawaiian salt, because what’s going to happen is that salt is going to melt into the ‘ahi, and it’s going to be perfect. The sauces in this recipe are the perfect combination with this fish and tomatoes and cucumbers.

Aloha Shoyu Poke Tower with ʻAhi, Salmon, and Avocado

Serves 4 to 6

Rice Layer
1 cup cooked rice, room temperature

Avocado Layer
1 ripe avocado, chopped

ʻAhi Poke
1 pound fresh ʻahi, cut into small cubes
½ teaspoon salt
½ cup minced onions
¼ cup minced green onions
⅓ cup chopped ogo
3 tablespoons Aloha Shoyu Poke Sauce

Salmon Poke
1 pound fresh salmon, cut into small cubes
½ teaspoon salt
½ cup minced red onions
¼ cup minced green onions
⅓ cup chopped ogo
2 tablespoons tobiko
3 tablespoons Aloha Shoyu Oyster Poke Sauce
¾ cup mayonnaise

Lomi Tomato
1 medium tomato, diced
2 tablespoons minced yellow onions
2 tablespoons minced red onions
1 tablespoon chopped green onions

Scan to watch Sam
make this dish!

Garnish
Tobiko, to taste
Sriracha, to taste

To make the 'Ahi Poke: In a mixing bowl, add 'ahi and salt. Mix well and let set for about 2 to 3 minutes. Add onions, green onions, ogo and Aloha Shoyu Poke Sauce. Mix well and chill.

To make the Salmon Poke: In a mixing bowl, add salmon and salt. Mix well and let set for about 2 to 3 minutes. Add onions, green onions, ogo, tobiko, and Aloha Shoyu Oyster Poke Sauce. Mix well. Add mayonnaise, mix well, and chill.

To make the Lomi Tomato: In a bowl, add tomato, yellow onions, red onions, green onions, and avocado. Mix well.

To assemble: On a plate, use a sushi mold to shape the bottom layer of rice. Add a layer of avocado followed by a layer of 'Ahi Poke, Salmon Poke, and Lomi Tomato. Use the back of a spoon to press each layer firmly. Carefully remove the mold, garnish with tobiko and a drizzle of sriracha, and enjoy!

Salmon Poke with Sensei Lettuce Cups

Serves 4

1½ pounds fresh Verlasso salmon, cubed
½ tablespoon pressed sesame seed oil
1 tablespoon Aloha Shoyu Tamari
2 tablespoons Ohana Flavors Korean Teriyaki Sauce
2 tablespoons Ohana Flavors Miso Sauce
2 tablespoons Ohana Flavors Shoyu Poke Sauce
1 Sensei Farms mini cucumber, diced
3 Sensei Farms Hawaiian hot peppers, minced
½ red onion, diced
1 head Sensei Farms romaine lettuce, separated into cups

Place all ingredients in a large mixing bowl (except lettuce). Toss to coat well. Spoon poke into lettuce cups and serve cold.

Our visit to Sensei Farms was amazing. Their locally-grown produce on Lānaʻi was so vibrant and beautiful, and we had the freshest farm-to-table experience. For this salmon poke, you could use white or yellow onions, but adding red onions gives the dish an extra pop of color. The hot peppers give this poke a really nice kick.

BYL AND BURNI LEONARD

If you've got tofu in the fridge, you can make tofu poke real quick. Get creative with what to add—see what you have in your fridge. The Leonard's had some watercress so we chopped up the stems. Here in Hawai'i, we're lucky to have Sumida's watercress farm. Raw watercress has a nice peppery taste that's similar to arugula.

Tofu Poke

Serves 2 to 4

1½ cups chopped watercress stems (reserve 1 tablespoon for dressing)
1 block firm tofu, cubed
⅔ bottle Aloha Shoyu Ume Shiso Dressing
1 package NOH Foods Poke Mix
½ teaspoon sesame oil
½ teaspoon honey

Garnish
2 teaspoons chopped green onions

Place watercress stems on a platter and spread evenly to form a base. Arrange the tofu cubes on the base. In a separate bowl, combine ume shiso dressing, poke mix, sesame oil, honey, and one tablespoon watercress stems. Mix well then pour mixture over tofu. Garnish with green onions.

Uncle Sam's Island-Style Tofu Poke

Serves 2 to 4

1 block firm tofu, drained and cut into 1-inch cubes
½ cup kim chee
1 tablespoon chopped green onions
1 tablespoon chopped red onions
6 cherry tomatoes, halved
½ avocado, cubed

Sauce
1½ cups Tanioka's Shoyu Poke Sauce
1 tablespoon kim chee juice
1 teaspoon Aloha Shoyu Soy Sauce
1 tablespoon Aloha Shoyu Kalbi Sauce
1 tablespoon chopped green onions
1 tablespoon chopped red onions

In a serving bowl, make a layer of half the tofu, then a layer of kim chee and top with the remaining tofu cubes. Add green onions, onions, tomatoes, and avocado.

Make Sauce by combining all ingredients; mix well. Pour sauce over tofu layers. Garnish with more onions, tomatoes, and kim chee.

I like to build this tofu with layers so you have a little bit of everything in one bite. This is a very refreshing poke that's plant-based, so it's good for you. And you can use some of the juice from the kim chee jar to add to the poke sauce to give it a little extra kick.

Kim Chee Tofu Poke

Serves 2 to 4

You don't need fish to make poke. If you have a block of tofu, you can start with that blank canvas and add whatever ingredients you have on hand like kim chee and tomatoes. Mix in some sauces and sesame oil and you have a super tasty tofu poke.

1 block firm tofu, drained
1 package Noh Poke Mix
1 tablespoon sesame oil
2 tablespoons chopped green onions
10 grape tomatoes, halved
1 tablespoon oyster sauce
3 tablespoons Aloha Shoyu Soy Sauce
3 tablespoons Noh Hula-Hula Sauce
1 teaspoon hot sauce
½ cup chopped kim chee

Garnish
Dried ʻōpae

Cut tofu into ¾-inch cubes and place in a bowl. Add poke mix, sesame oil, green onions, and tomatoes and toss. Add oyster sauce, soy sauce, Hula-Hula Sauce, hot sauce, and kim chee and mix well. Top with dried ʻōpae and serve.

FRANK DELIMA

Kim Chee Meatballs

Serves 4

1 pound ground beef
1 cup minced Halm's kim chee
1 tablespoon kim chee juice
1 tablespoon olive oil
2 heads baby bok choy, sliced
1 teaspoon Hawaiian Pride Char Siu Sauce
½ teaspoon Meyer lemon juice

In a large bowl, combine ground beef, minced kim chee, and kim chee juice and mix well. Roll mixture into meatballs.

In a skillet, heat the olive oil over medium-high heat and fry the meatballs until cooked through. Set aside. Using the same skillet, stir-fry baby bok choy until wilted. Add char siu sauce and lemon juice and mix well. Place bok choy on a platter, top with meatballs, and serve hot.

Local, legendary comedian Frank DeLima was a joy to visit. Even though his kitchen was small, what we made in there had big flavor. These meatballs are quick and easy to make. Adding the kim chee juice gives them that extra flavor. You can let the meat marinate in the kim chee for a few minutes before forming the meatballs. The kim chee has so much flavor, you don't need to add seasoning to the meatballs.

Scan to watch Sam
make this dish!

Korean Chicken Wings

Serves 4

Coating for Chicken
1 cup all-purpose flour
1 cup potato starch
2 tablespoons garlic salt

2 pounds chicken drumettes
Vegetable oil for deep-frying

Sauce
½ cup soy sauce
½ cup sugar
2 cloves garlic, minced
½ teaspoon black pepper
3 local chili peppers, remove and use seeds
4 stalks green onions, chopped

In a large bowl, mix together flour, starch, and garlic salt. Toss drumettes in coating mixture and deep fry in oil. Cook until golden brown. Remove and pat dry.

Mix Sauce ingredients well. Drench chicken wings in sauce. Enjoy!

Garlic Chicken Yogurt Kebabs

Serves 4

2 cups plain Greek yogurt
1 tablespoon minced garlic
Juice of 2 lemons
1 tablespoon paprika
Salt and pepper, to taste
3 to 4 pounds boneless and skinless chicken thighs, cut into 1½-inch pieces
1 red bell pepper, cut into 1½-inch pieces
1 yellow bell pepper, cut into 1½-inch pieces
1 red onion, cut into 1½-inch pieces
12 skewers (if using wooden skewers, soak them in water for 20 minutes before adding chicken and vegetables)
1 package quinoa (cooked according to package directions; can substitute water with chicken stock for more flavor)

Garnish
1 package mixed greens

In a bowl, combine yogurt, garlic, lemon juice, paprika, salt, and pepper. Add chicken, mix well, and marinate for 30 minutes.

Thread the chicken and vegetables onto the skewers. Grill kebabs until chicken is cooked through. Spoon quinoa on a platter, lay skewers on top of the quinoa, and garnish with mixed greens.

NOTE: *If you have extra chicken leftover, you can put it in a nice roasting pan and bake it in a 350°F oven anywhere between 35 to 45 minutes. Unbelievable.*

Kebabs make me think of summer barbecuing either at home or at the beach. They're a great party food because you can get creative mixing and matching proteins and vegetables and they travel well to a friend's house or to the beach. Use metal skewers because the metal skewers will help cook the chicken on the inside.

A lot of families in Hawai'i know what it's like to feed a lot of mouths on a budget. Frozen foods are great money and time-savers. Topping these tater tots with bacon, cream cheese, and a cilantro dip gives this appetizer a nice south-of-the-border flavor.

Baked Tater Tots with Bacon Cream Cheese and Cilantro Dip

Serves 2 to 4

1 bag tater tots, baked
¼ cup chopped cilantro (reserve 1 tablespoon for garnish)
1 (8-ounce) package cream cheese
½ cup shredded cheddar cheese
1 tablespoon milk
¼ cup bacon bits
Sriracha, to taste

Bake tater tots according to package directions until crisp. Place on a platter and garnish with cilantro.

In a saucepan, melt cream cheese and cheddar cheese together. Add milk to thin and remove from heat. Add remaining cilantro and bacon bits. Drizzle with sriracha and serve in a small bowl to use as a dipping sauce for the tater tots.

SOUPS AND SALADS

Canoe Crop Hawaiian Chowder

Serves 4 to 6

Spectrum

1 pound bacon, sliced
1½ cups diced onions
1½ cups diced celery
1 quart chicken stock
2 cups diced cooked ʻulu
2 cups diced Hilo purple sweet potato
1 cup fresh corn kernels
3 cups heavy cream
Salt and pepper, to taste

In a large pot, sauté bacon for 6 minutes. Add onions and celery and sauté for 5 minutes. Add chicken stock and simmer for 5 minutes. Add ʻulu, sweet potatoes, and corn and bring to a boil. Lower heat and bring to a simmer. Add heavy cream and season with salt and pepper. Stir well and serve.

OPTIONAL: *Add roux for a thicker consistency. To make a roux, it's equal parts butter and flour. In a saucepan, melt butter over medium high heat. Slowly whisk in flour until well-combined.* Cook for another 8 to 10 minutes and serve.

Scan to watch Sam make this dish!

Chicken Noodle Soup with Papaya & Cabbage

Serves 4

If you have leftover chicken and a box of chicken stock, this is a really quick soup you can make. You're just going to boil up some chicken stock and add the papayas like you would add pumpkin or squash—just right in the chicken stock.

½ box organic chicken stock
1 large green papaya, seeded and chopped
1 seasoned chicken breast, cooked and shredded
1 bunch bok choy stems, chopped
1 bunch choi sum stems, chopped
1 (8-ounce) package Tofu Shirataki Spaghetti noodles

In a large pot, heat chicken stock over medium-high heat and bring to a boil. Add papaya to soup and bring to a boil. Add chicken, bok choy stems, and choi sum stems and cook until vegetables are tender. Pour soup into a large bowl, top with noodles, and serve.

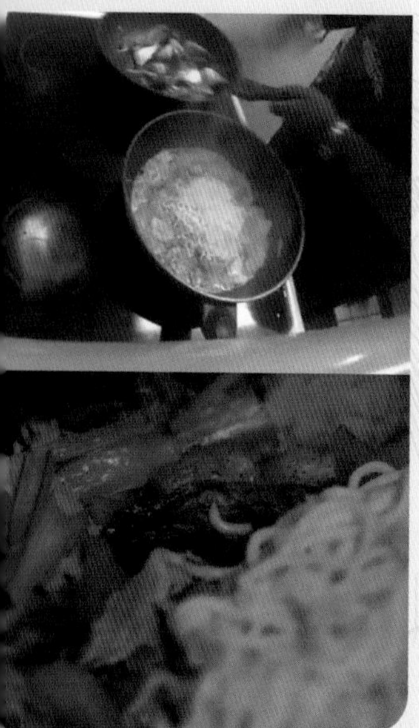

Fishcake Soup

Serves 4

- 2 cups chicken stock
- 2 fingers of fresh ginger, sliced
- 1 bunch cilantro, roughly chopped
- 1½ pounds fishcake, sliced
- ½ pound sugar snap peas
- 2 cups water
- ½ teaspoon salt
- 1 tablespoon green onions

In a large pot, heat chicken stock and water over medium-high heat. Add ginger, cilantro, and fishcake. Bring to a boil. Reduce heat and add sugar snaps. Season with salt to taste, garnish with green onions, and serve.

DWIGHT AND TRESE OTANI

We cooked up a feast when we visited the Otani's of D. Otani Produce. One of the dishes was this great soup. The fishcake we used was made fresh by Trese Otani's mom.

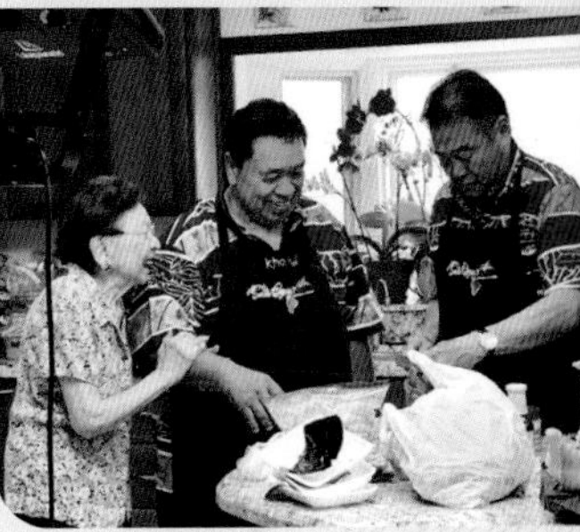

RUSSELL MARCHAN 'OHANA

Pig's Feet Soup

Serves 4

1 pound pig's feet
4 cloves garlic, crushed
2 tablespoons smashed ginger
1 stalk lemongrass, smashed and knotted
½ tomato, quartered
½ white onion, julienned
2 (14.5-ounce) cans chicken broth
1 large squash, cut into 2-inch pieces

Place pig's feet in a pressure cooker. Add garlic, ginger, lemongrass, tomato, onion, and chicken broth. Seal pressure cooker, set on high, and cook for 8 to 10 minutes.

Add squash and cook an additional 2 minutes. Pour soup into a large bowl and serve hot.

This is something I learned when I was a kid helping my parents in the kitchen: If you crush the lemongrass stalk with your hand and tie it into a knot, it will get more flavor out. Just drop the knotted bundle into the soup and let it do its thing.

Fruit Salad

Serves 4

Japanese pears are one of the many delicious fruits that we're lucky to have in Hawai‘i. This fruit salad can be served as a fresh side or enjoyed as a healthy snack. All of the fruits listed in this recipe can be substituted according to your preferences or with whatever you have at home. It's a nice reminder that throwing together a fruit salad can be simple.

1 cup blackberries, halved
1 cup strawberries, halved
1 cup blueberries
1 cup cherries
1 cup Japanese pear, diced

Garnish
Fresh spinach leaves

Cut blackberries and strawberries in half. Add blueberries, cherries, and diced Japanese pear and mix. Garnish with fresh spinach leaves.

CHAD KALELE AND JOANNE MCCOMBER

The Johnny's Delight Salad Dressing, which we named on the show, is made with some unexpected condiments, but stuff you can find in almost every fridge. Pair that with some avocado. The Big Island has some of the best.

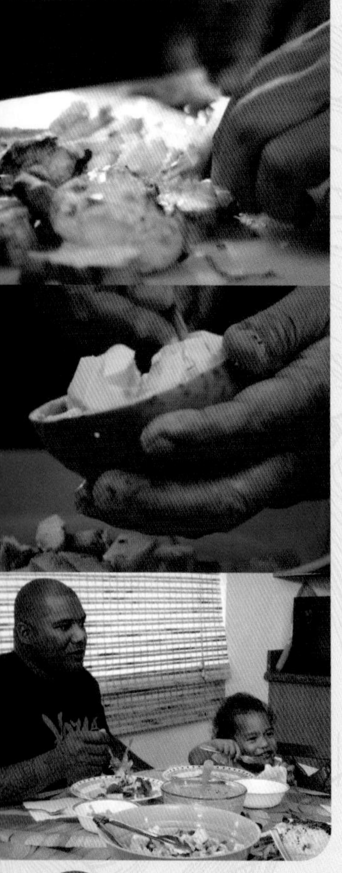

Chicken Avocado Salad with "Johnny's Delight" Dressing

Serves 2

Organic mixed greens
1 cup broccoli florets
6 to 8 asparagus spears
6 to 8 green beans, chopped
6 to 8 grape tomatoes, halved
2 to 3 cups sliced grilled chicken
1 small avocado, cubed

Johnny's Delight Salad Dressing
6 tablespoons Real Kraft Mayo
3 tablespoons Heinz Classic Sweet & Thick BBQ Sauce
1 tablespoon sweet chili sauce
1 tablespoon pineapple salsa
Sriracha, to taste

Place mixed greens in a large serving bowl. Add broccoli, asparagus, green beans, and tomatoes. Top with grilled chicken and avocado. Mix dressing ingredients together. Drizzle with Johnny's Delight Salad Dressing and serve.

MARIA OLIPAS AND TINA OSCAR

Chow Mein Salad

Serves 4

1 (12-ounce) package chow mein noodles
1 head romaine lettuce, chopped
1 cup leftover teriyaki beef
1 cup daikon kim chee

Special Dressing
3 tablespoons Aloha Shoyu Soy Sauce
1 teaspoon brown sugar
1 teaspoon sesame oil
1 teaspoon fresh lemon juice
1 teaspoon citrus honey
1 teaspoon kim chee juice
Black pepper, to taste

Place chow mein (cold) in a mixing bowl. Add chopped romaine lettuce. Toss well then place on a serving platter. Place teriyaki beef on chow mein/romaine mixture and garnish with daikon kim chee.

Combine Special Dressing ingredients, mix well, and drizzle over salad.

When you have leftover beef, all you have to do is reheat it. You don't want to overcook it. A good way to serve leftover beef is in a salad. This chow mein salad has some great flavor with a citrusy dressing that's got some kim chee kick to it. It's a nice way to start a meal.

DUSTIN AND TARA ALFORD

A local favorite, soba is a Japanese noodle made with buckwheat flour, usually served cold with a soy dressing. This soba salad is light and fresh.

Soba Salad

Serves 2

1 (8-ounce) package soba noodles, cooked
2 cucumbers, sliced
1 block firm tofu, drained and diced
1 (5.5-ounce) package Japanese fishcake (kamaboko), sliced
1 cup bean sprouts

Garnish
¼ cup green onions

Place noodles on a serving platter. Arrange cucumber slices around the edges. Layer tofu, fishcake, and bean sprouts on top. Garnish with green onions. Serve with your choice of sesame or soy dressing.

Poke Somen Salad

Serves 4

1 (16-ounce) package somen noodles
1 (11-ounce) package mixed greens
2 containers poke
1 medium tomato, diced
1 tablespoon green onions
Aloha Shoyu Shiso Ume Dressing
Goma (sesame) sauce

In a large pot, bring water to a boil. Add somen noodles and cook as directed. Place noodles in a strainer and place in an ice bath. Once somen noodles are cooled down, drain liquid and set aside.

In a salad bowl, layer mixed greens, somen noodles, and poke. Top with tomatoes and green onions. Drizzle with shiso ume dressing and goma sauce.

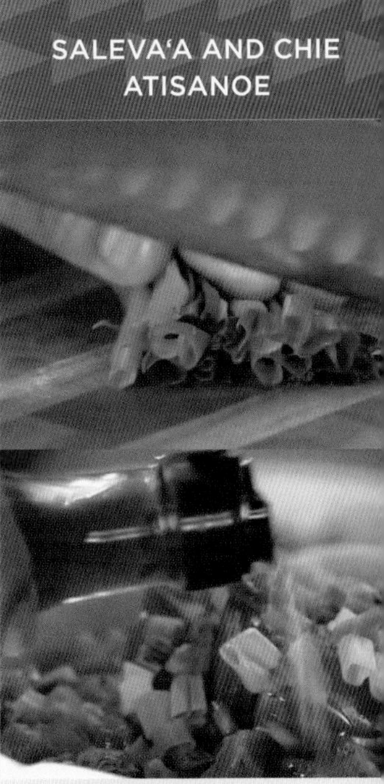

Unlike the thicker kishimen noodles we fry in the Konishiki-Fun recipe, in this recipe we want to cool the somen noodles down in an ice bath after cooking, because we want to serve the noodles cold. This is meant to be served cold as a nice, refreshing, light salad perfect for hot summer days.

Canoe Crop Salad

Serves 4

2 cups chopped Okinawan sweet potatoes
½ kabocha, chopped
2 cups chopped Hawai'i 'Ulu Cooperative 'Ulu Breadfruit Quarters
2 cups chopped Hawai'i 'Ulu Cooperative Kalo (Taro)
2 carrots, grated
3 stalks celery, chopped
4 boiled eggs, peeled and chopped
2 cups mayonnaise
1 teaspoon garlic salt
1 teaspoon black pepper
1 bag baby spinach, bruised

I call this a canoe crop salad because it uses 'ulu, kalo, and sweet potatoes. The first Polynesians to come to Hawai'i brought these plants with them and they became a staple of the Hawaiian diet. This is one of my favorite potato salads to make. And here's a trick to make the boiled eggs look crumbled: hold the peeled egg in the palm of your hand and with your other hand, use a fork to gently poke the side of the egg and pull down causing the egg to crumble.

In a large pot, bring water to a boil. Lower heat and add sweet potatoes, kabocha, 'ulu, and taro. Cook for 10 to 15 minutes or until tender. Remove from water and drain well. Once cooled, place ingredients in a large bowl and combine with carrots, celery, eggs, mayonnaise, garlic salt, and black pepper. Lastly, add spinach and mix well.

KAI LENNY

These steaks are super simple and super tasty. Just season with salt and pepper. That's it. We got creative with the salad dressing. You may have never thought of using a haupia pudding mix in a dressing, but it works! You don't have to go to a lot of trouble to make a nice dressing. If you've got some prepared mixes and sauces in the pantry or fridge, get creative and try combining them. Keep your flavors balanced with salty and sweet and add a little acid for that tang.

Steak Salad with Coconut Dressing

Serves 4

2 steaks
½ teaspoon salt
½ teaspoon black pepper
½ tablespoon olive oil
1 package mixed greens
¼ onion, thinly sliced
½ red bell pepper, julienned
1 package mixed greens (for plating)

Coconut Dressing
1 packet NOH Foods Coconut Pudding (Haupia) Mix
½ cup 2 Chicks Backyard Juice or chili pepper water
½ cup Aloha Shoyu Mango and Pineapple Sauce
1 tablespoon Maille Whole Grain Dijon Mustard

Season both sides of the steaks with salt and pepper. In a large skillet, add olive oil over medium-high heat. Cook steaks for 5 minutes. Flip and cook for additional 5 minutes for medium rare. Remove from heat and let rest for 5 minutes.

Build your salad with the mixed greens, onion, and bell pepper. To make the dressing, combine all ingredients in a small bowl and mix well. Drizzle dressing over salad. Slice the steak and serve alongside the salad.

Island-Style Seared ‘Ahi Salad

Serves 4

3 (6-ounce) fresh ‘ahi blocks (marinated in 1 tablespoon miso and 1 tablespoon teriyaki sauce)
3 cups lettuce
1 tomato, sliced
1 cucumber, sliced
1 large tortilla bowl

Asian Vinaigrette
3 tablespoons rice wine vinegar
3 tablespoons tamari
2 tablespoons olive oil
1 tablespoon honey
1 tablespoon finely diced cilantro

Garnish
Fresh cilantro sprigs
Edible flowers (optional)

In a shallow dish, combine miso and teriyaki sauce. Coat ‘ahi blocks with mixture and marinate for 1 hour.

In a skillet over high heat, sear each side of the ‘ahi blocks.

Mix Asian Vinaigrette ingredients until well-combined.

In a bowl, add lettuce, tomatoes, and cucumbers and toss in vinaigrette. Place lettuce mixture in a fried tortilla bowl and top with seared ‘ahi. Garnish with cilantro and edible flowers.

GOVERNOR JOSH GREEN

I like using our Big Island fish. When we made this dish with Governor Josh Green, we used fresh ‘ahi and local greens from the Big Island and one of my favorite Asian vinaigrettes that’s light and fresh. For fun, we served it in a large tortilla bowl, or tostada bowl. You can buy these in grocery stores.

MICHAEL AND KEHAU KAUAKAHI

Use up your leftover poi in a reimagined salad dressing. Even if it isn't fresh poi, you can still use it. It sounds crazy but it tastes great. Remember, these recipes are all about improvising and using what you've got on hand in the kitchen.

Salmon Salad with Poi Dressing

Serves 4 to 8

½ (11-ounce) package mixed greens
8 small salmon fillets, cooked and seasoned with garlic salt, pepper and ʻalaea sea salt

Poi Dressing
4 tablespoons poi
1 cup Aloha Shoyu Black Sesame Dressing
1 teaspoon chili pepper water

Place mixed greens on a platter. Arrange salmon fillets on bed of greens.

Combine Poi Dressing ingredients and mix well. Drizzle dressing over salmon and serve.

Salad Niçoise

Serves 2 to 4

Dressing with Taco Bell Taco Seasoning Mix
3 to 4 tablespoons Greek dressing
½ package Taco Bell Taco Seasoning Mix
1 teaspoon water
2 to 3 tablespoons Kraft Classic Ranch dressing

3 to 4 cups lettuce or spring mix
1 cucumber, julienned
1 small salmon fillet, cooked and flaked
1 small 'ahi fillet, cooked and sliced
1 small lobster tail, cooked and chopped
½ sweet potato, cooked and sliced
½ tomato, seeded and chopped

Whisk dressing ingredients together until blended.

Place lettuce on a serving dish. Arrange the cucumbers, salmon, 'ahi, lobster, sweet potato, and tomato on top of greens. Drizzle with dressing and serve.

If you have just one or two servings of different fish, you can stretch them out by building a nice salad. All you need is a bag of spring mix and whatever vegetables you may have on hand. You can turn a simple salad into a layered salad like this one. And, yes, you read that right: we made a dressing using Taco Bell seasoning!

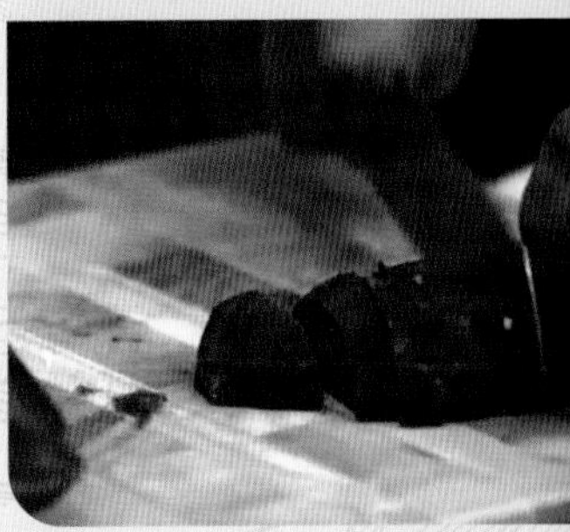

If you've got tofu, a variety of vegetables, and lettuce mix, you can put together a really nice salad. The wow factor is the dressing. This vinaigrette uses Lānaʻi Honey and boy does it make a nice dressing. Fresh herbs also add a lot of flavor. If you can, try keeping a small herb garden in your kitchen. It makes a difference and is economical.

Tofu Salad
with Lānaʻi Honey Ginger Vinaigrette

Serves 2 to 4

1 block tofu, drained and cubed
Salt and pepper, to taste
1 tablespoon cornstarch
2 tablespoons olive oil
2 containers Sensei Farms Lānaʻi Mix
2 Sensei Farms tomatoes, cut into wedges
2 Sensei Farms mini cucumbers, sliced
1 medium red onion, sliced

Lānaʻi Honey Ginger Vinaigrette Dressing
3 tablespoons Dijon mustard
3 tablespoons Lānaʻi honey
½ cup olive oil
½ cup red wine vinegar
2½ tablespoons minced ginger
1 tablespoon chopped Sensei Farms Genovese basil
1 tablespoon chopped Sensei Farms purple basil
Pinch of salt

Season tofu with salt and pepper and coat with cornstarch. Heat olive oil in a skillet and cook over medium-high heat until all sides are golden brown. Set aside.

To make the dressing, combine all ingredients and mix well.

Assemble salad by placing lettuce mix on a platter and top with tofu, tomatoes, cucumbers, and onions. Drizzle with vinaigrette dressing and serve.

Jabong Vinaigrette Dressing

Serves 4

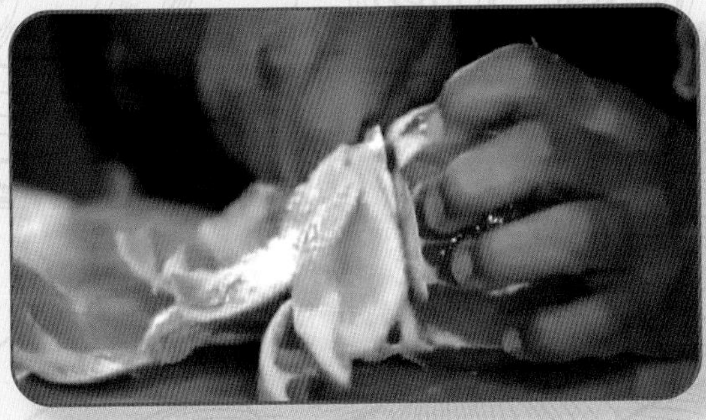

1 jabong
2 tablespoons vinegar
2 tablespoons Dijon mustard
2 tablespoons honey
½ cup olive oil
Black pepper, to taste

Peel jabong, divide into sections, and squeeze juice into a mixing bowl. Chop squeezed sections and add to bowl. Add vinegar, Dijon mustard, honey, olive oil, and pepper. Whisk until ingredients are combined. Serve over vegetables and greens of your choice.

Jabong, pamplemousse, or pomelo, is one of Hawai'i's favorite fruits. Sweet like an orange, jabong is used in a variety of dishes. The thick skin and bitter pith can be tricky, but once separated into segments, the flesh makes a nice treat. The sour juice mixed with sweet honey adds a complex flavor profile to a traditionally simple dressing.

Kaffir Lime Leaf Vinaigrette

Serves 4

1 cup white vinegar
2 tablespoons Dijon mustard
¼ cup honey
½ teaspoon minced garlic
½ teaspoon Himalayan salt
1 tablespoon Aloha Shoyu Hawaiian Honey Glaze
1 tablespoon Aloha Shoyu Kalbi Sauce
¼ cup olive oil
1 tablespoon chopped kaffir lime leaves

In a blender, add vinegar, Dijon mustard, honey, minced garlic, Himalayan salt, honey glaze, kalbi sauce, and olive oil. Blend all the ingredients until everything is mixed. Once you've blended all ingredients, add chopped kaffir lime leaves and blend. Prepare your favorite salad, drizzle with dressing, and enjoy!

Kaffir limes don't have a lot of juice; it's the zest and leaves that are commonly used in Asian cooking. The kaffir lime has a really nice, intense fragrance—it's kind of like eating a bouquet of something that smells good. You can pour the vinaigrette in a bottle and store it in the fridge. Or, you can add an egg yolk and make it really creamy and thick.

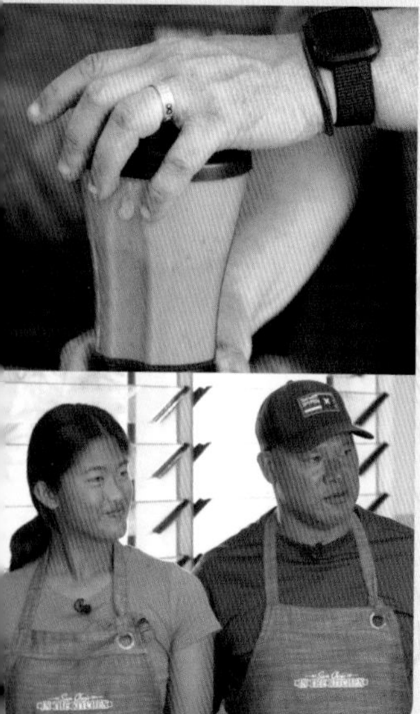

SIDES

Irish soda bread is a quick bread to make. It's a dense bread and it goes great with the Guinness Lamb Stew on page 84.

Crusty Irish Soda Bread

Serves 4

2 cups all-purpose flour
3 tablespoons sugar
½ teaspoon baking soda
1½ teaspoons baking powder
½ teaspoon salt
⅓ cup raisins
¼ cup cold unsalted butter, cut into small cubes
¾ cup buttermilk

Preheat oven to 400°F. Line a baking pan with parchment paper.

In a large mixing bowl, combine flour, sugar, baking soda, baking powder, salt, and raisins. Cut the cold butter cubes into the flour mixture. Add buttermilk and knead the dough until combined. Form the dough into a ball and place in the lined baking pan. Bake for 30 minutes or until the crust is golden brown.

Burrata with Tropical Fruit Salsa

Serves 4

½ cup diced strawberries
½ cup diced pineapple
½ cup diced mango
3 tablespoons diced red onions
Fresh cilantro, reserve some for garnish
1 tablespoon olive oil
Pinch of salt and pepper
Pinch of cumin
1 tablespoon miso sauce
3 to 4 large pineapple slices
2 balls of burrata cheese
Balsamic glaze

Garnish
Cilantro sprigs

In a bowl, add strawberries, pineapple, mango, onions, cilantro, olive oil, salt, pepper, and cumin. Mix well. Add miso sauce, mix, and set aside.

Place pineapple slices on serving plate and spoon fruit salsa on top of pineapple, reserving some to use as final topping. Place balls of burrata cheese on top of salsa and top with remaining salsa. Drizzle everything with balsamic glaze and garnish with cilantro.

Miso really can be added to just about anything. You would never think to add it to fruit, but it makes this dish a nice savory salsa. And the burrata cheese is like the two best things, mozzarella and cream. So it's fresh mozzarella mixed with cream stuffed inside more mozzarella. It's delicious.

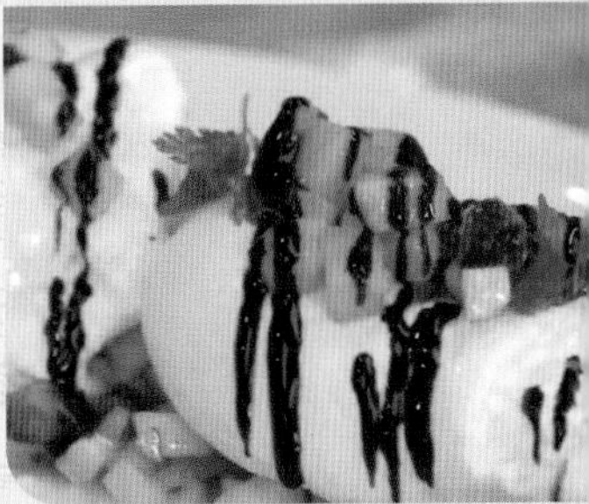

DUSTIN AND TARA ALFORD

Spanish Rice

Serves 4

3 to 4 tablespoons olive oil
1 pound ground turkey
1 package taco seasoning
3 to 4 cups cooked rice
½ onion, chopped
½ cup chopped olives
½ cup sliced green beans
½ cup chopped fresh cilantro (reserve 1 tablespoon for garnish)
¼ cup bacon bits
½ teaspoon garlic powder
Chili powder, to taste

Garnish
¼ cup shredded cheese

Leftover rice is probably the number one item in everybody's fridge in Hawai'i. Try something new and turn it into Spanish rice. Add taco seasoning, ground turkey, and chopped veggies for a rich, smoky, one-pan meal.

In a skillet, cook ground turkey in olive oil on medium-high heat. Add taco seasoning and cook as directed. Add rice, onions, olives, green beans, cilantro, bacon bits, garlic powder, and chili powder. Cook until onions are soft.

Place on a serving platter and top with shredded cheese and cilantro.

Z's Casserole

Serves 2

2 cups mashed potatoes, prepared
1½ tablespoons Kraft Shredded Mild Cheddar Cheese
2½ tablespoons pumpkin purée
3 grape tomatoes, halved
Dash of olive oil
Black pepper, to taste

Preheat oven to 325°F.

In a medium bowl, combine mashed potatoes and cheddar cheese. Set aside.

Halve the pumpkin purée and spoon into 2 mini casserole dishes and flatten. Halve potato and cheese mixture and spoon into each dish on top of the pumpkin purée. Top off with more shredded cheese. Garnish with tomatoes. Season with olive oil and pepper. Bake for 20 to 25 minutes.

ERAN, BARBEA AND ZEZA GANOT

Dress up some leftover mashed potatoes by mixing in cheese. Then take it up a notch and make a layered casserole with pumpkin purée. Super easy, super quick.

Country Hash

Serves 2

Cube leftover potatoes and make a hash. You know, potatoes have a lot of sugar in them, so the first thing that will happen is the sugar is going to start browning over the heat which extracts flavor. Caramelize everything until it's a nice golden brown.

1 teaspoon of olive oil
1 medium-sized potato, cubed
1 cup chopped brussels sprouts
½ cup sliced mushrooms
½ cup julienned onions
½ cup chopped cooked bacon
¼ cup dried cranberries
Handful of Chex cereal, crushed

Add 1 teaspoon of olive oil to a medium pan. Add potatoes, brussels sprouts, mushrooms, onions, bacon, and cranberries and caramelize all ingredients over a medium-high heat.

Remove from heat and garnish with crushed Chex cereal.

Corned Beef Hash

Serves 2 to 4

3½ tablespoons olive oil
1 medium red onion, diced
1 small red bell pepper, seeded and diced
1 small green bell pepper, seeded and diced
2 Okinawan sweet potatoes, boiled and cubed
4 Yukon gold potatoes, boiled and cubed
2 pounds corned beef, cooked and cut into small pieces
½ teaspoon salt

In a large skillet, heat olive oil. Add onions and bell peppers. Add potatoes. Cook and allow the bottom layer to crisp. Carefully mix in the corned beef and season with salt. Continue to turn over the mixture allowing it to crisp in between until the ingredients are cooked.

In a hash, you want to crust the bottom, so it gets nice and crispy. You don't want it soggy. You want it crispy because that's what makes it 'ono. So once you put all the ingredients in the pan, let it sit a bit so the bottom gets nice and crispy.

JUSTIN CRUZ

Savory Bread Pudding

Serves 4

Day-old, leftover bread screams bread pudding. It's the perfect way to use up old bread, and it doesn't have to be a sweet bread pudding. You can make a savory one. This recipe is a fun one because we added chopped pears.

5 slices bread
1 cup chopped broccoli
6 eggs
1 tablespoon Parmesan cheese
1 cup chopped pears
2 tablespoons minced green onions
2 to 3 tablespoons ranch dressing
1 pinch salt
1 pinch black pepper
1 pinch garlic salt
½ cup water

Preheat oven to 350°F.

Break up bread slices and place in a glass baking pan. In a bowl, combine all remaining ingredients except water, mix well, and pour over bread pieces.

Add water to a large baking pan (to help steam/poach the egg mixture) and place the glass pan in the middle. Bake for 45 minutes.

Holiday Stuffing

Serves 4 to 6

½ stick butter
3 tablespoons olive oil
1 Portuguese sausage, diced
1 cup diced onion
1 cup diced celery
½ cup diced carrot
1 bag fresh spinach
2 boxes Stove Top stuffing mix, uncooked
1 box chicken stock
Salt and pepper, to taste

Add butter and olive oil in a pot. Sauté Portuguese sausage, onions, celery, and carrots until vegetables are tender. Add spinach and cook for 3 to 5 minutes. Add ¼ cup of the chicken stock and stir. Add Stove Top stuffing mix and combine well. Slowly add chicken stock until you get your desired consistency. Season with salt and pepper.

The challenging part of making a holiday meal is making all the sides. But you don't have to make everything from scratch. This is my family's recipe for an easy stuffing. I'm just elevating boxed stuffing with a *mirepoix* of onion, celery, and carrots. The carrots add a little sweetness and nice color to it.

Chicken
Sea
CORNED BEEF

HI-EMA Surf and Turf Patties

Serves 4

1 cup cooked rice
1 can Vienna sausage
1 can Spam, minced
1 can corned beef
1 can tuna
½ Portuguese sausage, minced
1 small onion, chopped
¼ cup chopped chives
3 eggs
Cooking oil

In a large bowl, add cooked rice, Vienna sausage, Spam, corned beef, tuna, Portuguese sausage, onions, chives, and eggs. Mix well and form into patties.

In a skillet, heat cooking oil over medium heat. Fry patties until golden brown. Flip over and cook until golden brown.

HAWAI'I EMERGENCY MANAGEMENT AGENCY

We visited the Hawai'i Emergency Management Agency to help them promote the importance of hurricane readiness in the islands. This recipe utilizes some shelf-stable food we're all familiar with here in the islands like Spam and Vienna sausage. It's quick and easy to make and can be made on a portable grill (make sure you know whether your grill is safe to use indoors or if it's only safe for outdoor use).

CHRIS IWAMURA AND KIM SHIGEMASA

Create a stuffing with leftover rice and vegetables. Portobello mushrooms are large enough to hold stuffing and can be a great side dish or a satisfying vegetarian main dish.

Stuffed Portobello Mushrooms

Serves 4 to 6

2 tablespoons butter
6 large portobello mushrooms (remove and finely chop stems and gills)
Salt and pepper, to taste
2 shallots, finely chopped
4 garlic cloves, minced
1 cup cooked kale
1 cup cooked spinach
2 cups cooked and seasoned basmati rice
Juice of ½ lemon
1 teaspoon balsamic vinegar
½ cup finely grated Parmesan cheese

Garnish
Olakai Sea Asparagus

Preheat oven to 350°F.

In a skillet, melt butter over medium heat. Season the mushroom caps with salt and pepper and sauté topside down for a few minutes. Set mushroom caps aside.

In the same skillet, sauté chopped mushroom stems and gills, shallots, garlic, kale, spinach, rice, and lemon juice. Remove from heat and add balsamic vinegar and cheese. Mix well. Stuff the mushroom caps with mixture and place on a baking sheet. Bake for 10 to 15 minutes.

Veggie-Stuffed Peppers

Serves 4

2 bell peppers, seeded and halved
½ cup chopped carrots
½ cup corn kernels
½ cup chopped zucchini
½ cup chopped onions
½ cup chopped tomatoes
½ cup chopped broccoli
1 tablespoon chopped garlic
1 tablespoon Aloha Shoyu Soy Sauce
2 tablespoons Parmesan cheese
Salt, to taste
1 cup panko
Olive oil
4 cheese slices, sliced diagonally

Preheat oven to 350°F.

In a skillet over medium-high heat, cook peppers for a few minutes to soften. Remove peppers from skillet and arrange them in a baking dish.

In the same skillet, add all the vegetables, soy sauce, Parmesan cheese, and salt. Sauté veggie mixture until al dente. Add panko to absorb liquid and bind the veggies. Spoon veggie mixture into pepper halves. Top with cheese and bake until cheese is melted.

Panko can transform runny dishes into culinary delights. It's a versatile ingredient that adds depth and texture and acts as a binder. You'll see that when you sauté all the vegetables together, they release a lot of water. The panko will absorb all the liquid and bind everything together.

Kakuma comes from young unfurled hapu'u (native Hawaiian tree fern) shoots, which can be found in Puna's rainforests on the Big Island during the spring. You can buy cleaned and ready-to-eat Kakuma in local markets. It's delicious pickled or pan-fried like in this recipe where we mixed things up with 'ukulele virtuoso Jake Shimabukuro and gave it a BBQ flair.

Big Island Kakuma with Tofu

Serves 2 to 4

2 cups water
1½ cups sliced kakuma
1 tablespoon Halm's Hawaiian BBQ Sauce
1 tablespoon Aloha Shoyu Soy Sauce
1½ block firm tofu, cut into 1-inch cubes
1 teaspoon sliced green onions and 2 kale leaves for garnish

In a skillet, bring water to a simmer. Add kakuma, Hawaiian BBQ Sauce, and Aloha Shoyu. Bring to a boil and allow kakuma to absorb the flavors of the sauces.

Add tofu and braise for 5 to 8 minutes. Garnish with sliced green onions and kale leaves.

NOTE: *From the Department of Horticulture, Cooperative Extension Service, College of Tropical Agriculture and Human Resources, University of Hawaii at Mānoa—"Kakuma is prepared from spineless young unfurled hapu'u (native Hawaiian tree fern) shoots. The shoots are cut into 4-6" pieces. Remove any hairs and boil till the center turns maroon. It is recommended to boil kakuma outdoors, as it produces acrid fumes. The green skin is removed leaving the maroon centers which are placed into a bowl of clean, cool water. The pieces must be rinsed and the water changed daily. The kakuma is ready for consumption when the soaked water is clear and no longer stained tan in color. This process which takes at least a few days, removes the acidic bitterness. The cleaned kakuma should be kept in water which is changed daily and refrigerated until use. Cleaned kakuma is sold in local markets and Chinatown. Kakuma is delicious pickled or pan-fried with pork."*

Pan-Fried ʻUlu

Serves 2 to 4

1 medium ʻulu, firm and ripe
Water to cover ʻulu
Salt, to taste
1 Hawaiian chili pepper, minced
3 cups flour
1 block butter

Peel ʻulu and cut into steaks. Place in a large pot and cover with water; add salt and chili pepper. Bring to a boil and cook until tender (about 25 minutes). Remove ʻulu from pot and dry on paper towels.

After ʻulu has cooled, lightly coat pieces in flour. In a sauté pan, melt butter over medium heat. Add the flour-dusted ʻulu and sauté in melted butter until light brown on all sides.

Brought to Hawaiʻi by Polynesian voyagers, ʻulu (breadfruit) can be difficult to work with because of how seasonal they are and the effort it takes to prepare them, but anything you can do with a potato you can do with ʻulu. And now, we're lucky the have frozen, fully prepared ʻulu available in stores across the island—no peeling, slicing, or dicing required. Just open up the bag.

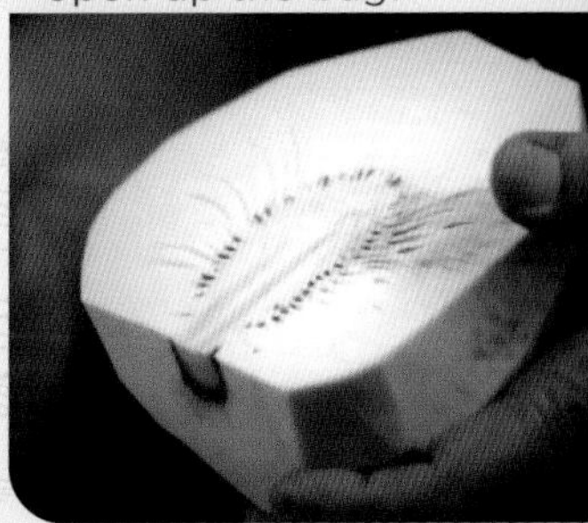

Soft Tofu with Pan-Roasted Vegetables

Serves 4

2 tablespoons olive oil
½ block soft tofu, cut in half
Sweet peppers (red and yellow) cut into strips
1 bunch gai lan (Chinese broccoli), rinsed and stems split
1 medium red onion, cut into strips
1½ tablespoons Aloha Shoyu Soy Sauce
1 tablespoon Aloha Shoyu Ponzu Sauce

In a sauté pan, heat olive oil over medium heat. Add tofu and vegetables and cook for 5 minutes. Season with soy sauce and a splash of ponzu sauce. Mix well and serve hot.

For Queen's Health Systems' tenth anniversary, we whipped up this flavorful soft tofu medley featuring ali'i mushrooms, kohlrabi, and pan-seared peppers. Kohlrabi is part of the mustard family and tastes similar to the broccoli stalk but is more sweet and tender.

Oven-Roasted Vegetables

Serves 4

1 bag asparagus, trimmed
1 bag brussels sprouts
2 medium red onions
1 medium tomato
1 carton mushrooms
1 cup olive oil
Salt, to taste (about 1 tablespoon)
½ teaspoon white or black pepper
½ cup barbecue sauce
½ cup Italian dressing

Preheat oven to 350°F.

Trim asparagus by removing the bottoms (about 1 or 2 inches). Clean brussels sprouts and cut in half. Cut red onions in half and slice into half rings. Cut tomato in half and slice into half rings. Clean mushrooms and slice.

Place vegetables in a baking dish and drizzle with olive oil and season with salt and pepper. Cook for 15 to 20 minutes or until al dente.

Mix barbecue sauce and Italian dressing together and drizzle over vegetables.

NOTE: *Don't throw away the trimmed bottoms of asparagus. Save them and use them in a cream soup.*

Oven roasting makes veggies taste delicious while maintaining all the nutrients, and these veggies are the perfect, healthy side.

MAIN DISHES

KALEHUA AH SOON

This sukiyaki recipe shows that you don't need a lot of ingredients on hand to make a quick, flavorful dish. The cook is really fast because the beef is thinly sliced and you want the onions to keep a bit of their crunch. The whiskey adds a nice flavor profile.

Marinated Beef Sukiyaki

Serves 4

1 pound beef, thinly sliced
5 cloves garlic, finely chopped
½ onion, finely sliced
1 tablespoon Aloha Shoyu Soy Sauce
1½ tablespoons whiskey
1 teaspoon seasoning salt
1 tablespoon avocado oil
Pepper, to taste

In a bowl, add beef, garlic, onions, soy sauce, whiskey, and seasoning salt. Mix and let marinate for 20 minutes.

In a skillet, heat oil over medium-high heat. Add marinated beef and pepper. Pan fry until medium-rare and serve hot.

Guava Jam Glazed Steak

Serves 3

3 steaks
1½ tablespoons Aloha Shoyu Soy Sauce
1½ tablespoons Mr. Yoshida's Sauce
3 to 4 cloves garlic, minced
1 tablespoon olive oil
1½ tablespoons guava jam

Garnish
2 tablespoons green onions

Remove steaks from container/tray they came in, pour the sauces into the tray, and put steaks back into container to marinate. Let one side marinate for a few minutes, then flip so the other side can marinate. Top that side with garlic.

Heat a pan on high heat. Sear steak on both sides. Add olive oil. Pour the leftover marinade over steaks. Add guava jam to the pan to glaze steaks.

Remove steaks from pan, let rest a few minutes then slice steaks and place on a serving dish. Pour the cooked juices in the pan over the steaks and garnish with green onions. This is great served with rice or could be served as a pūpū.

NOTE: *Save time and a dish by marinating the steaks inside the package they came in. Just open the package, remove the steaks, pour Aloha Shoyu inside the bottom tray, and put the steaks back in. Easy.*

Any flavor of jam can be a fantastic glaze for grilled meat, and here in Hawai'i we have a lot of local jams to choose from. Add the jam during the final stages of cooking so you don't risk wasting or burning the glaze. Once off the grill, you can add a final coat as the meat rests which will give the steak an added burst of flavor.

GLENNA MARAS
AND DANA PALUMBO

I like making hash like this because it's very tasty and you can add a nice fried egg on top, Indonesian-style. For this hash, we used leftover juicy cuts of steak made by Glenna's husband, and then tossed it with hearty potatoes and bell peppers. It's a satisfying dish that's perfect for any meal of the day.

Asian Steak Hash

Serves 4

½ cup chopped sweet peppers
½ cup minced red onion
6 mushrooms, sliced
3 cloves fresh garlic, minced
3 to 4 cooked potatoes, diced
4 (6-ounce) cooked steaks, diced
2 tablespoons soy sauce
1 tablespoon miso sauce
Salt and pepper, to taste
3 eggs, fried

Garnish
2 tablespoons flat leaf parsley
Sriracha

In a skillet, cook sweet peppers, onions, mushrooms, and garlic until tender. Add potatoes and combine well. Cook for several minutes until the potatoes are heated through. Add steak, soy sauce, and miso sauce. Top hash with fried eggs and garnish with parsley and sriracha.

LOIS HUNTER AND MIKE MORGAN

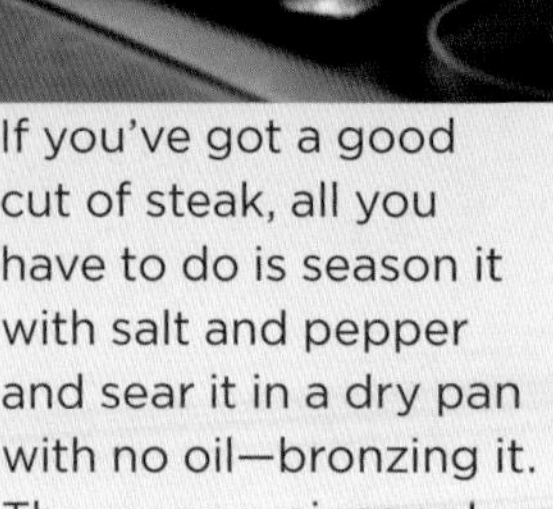

If you've got a good cut of steak, all you have to do is season it with salt and pepper and sear it in a dry pan with no oil—bronzing it. The mango-pineapple glaze adds a nice tropical flavor.

Bronzed Steaks with Truffle Oil

Serves 4

4 steaks
Salt and pepper, to taste
½ cup Aloha Shoyu Mango Pineapple Teriyaki Glaze
1 cup sliced fresh mushrooms
1 cup halved cherry tomatoes
2 tablespoons truffle oil

Season steaks with salt and pepper and cook over high heat. Pan sear for 5 to 6 minutes for medium rare. Remove from heat and let rest. Deglaze the same pan with teriyaki glaze, mushrooms, tomatoes, and truffle oil.

Pour mixture into a small bowl and serve on the side. Slice steaks, drizzle with truffle oil and serve.

Grilled Steak Stir-Fry

Serves 2

1 steak, prepared with salt, pepper, and Montreal steak seasoning, cooked to medium doneness, sliced into pieces about ½-inch thick
1 onion, sliced
4 mushrooms, sliced lengthwise
4 tablespoons yakiniku sauce
2 tablespoons oyster sauce
2 tablespoons mushroom soy sauce

Garnish
¼ cup chopped cilantro
¼ cup chopped green onions

Add cooked steak to hot skillet. Add onions. Stir until slightly opaque. Add mushrooms. Stir until tender. Add yakiniku sauce, oyster sauce, and mushroom soy sauce. Stir to combine. Remove from heat.

Garnish with cilantro and green onions.

If you have one, nicely cooked leftover steak and you want to stretch it into a meal for two, make a stir-fry with just a handful of ingredients. Cutting all the ingredients in a uniform size not only helps everything cook evenly, but it looks nicer when plated.

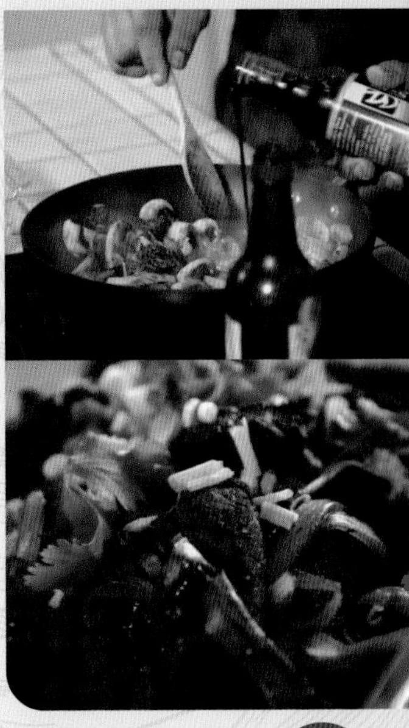

Steak is so much easier to cook than it seems. All you need is a good cut of meat. A rich and hearty meal, pan-fried steak and mushrooms is the kind of dish that encourages the whole family to gather at the table and enjoy their time together.

Pan-Fried Steak with Portobello Mushrooms

Serves 3 to 4

3 steaks
Garlic salt, to taste
3 Portobello mushrooms, sliced thick
3 tablespoons soy sauce

Season steaks with garlic salt. Sear steaks in a large skillet over medium-high heat. Cook for about 10 minutes on each side. Remove from heat and let them rest.

Cut steak into strips and put back into pan with mushrooms and soy sauce and cook until mushrooms are tender.

TIM AND MAYE KEPO'O

Steak Ziti

Serves 4

2½ cups uncooked pasta
1 jar red pasta sauce
½ teaspoon Italian seasoning
1 teaspoon minced garlic
½ teaspoon sugar
1 tablespoon olive oil
1 steak, cooked and chopped
5 cheese slices

Preheat oven to 350°F.

Cook pasta as directed. In a large bowl, mix pasta, sauce, Italian seasoning, garlic, and sugar. Pour mixture into a baking pan. In a skillet, heat olive oil over medium heat and reheat steak for 2 to 3 minutes. Place steak on top of pasta and lay cheese slices over steak. Bake for 20 minutes.

You can make this with any tube-shaped pasta you have on hand: ziti, macaroni, penne, rigatoni. And choose any cheese you want for the top. This is all about using leftovers and what you have on hand in your pantry and fridge.

Beef Tomato

Serves 2 to 4

½ medium onion, quartered
¾ cup chopped celery
½ cup water
½ cup teriyaki sauce
¾ cup diced tomatoes
1 cup quartered mushrooms
1 teaspoon sliced fresh ginger
5 cloves garlic, smashed
1 pound leftover grilled steak, sliced

Stir-fry onions and celery until soft. Add water and teriyaki sauce. Stir well. Add tomatoes, mushrooms, ginger, and garlic. Bring to a boil.

Make a slurry with equal parts cornstarch and water. Whisk slurry into stir-fry a little bit at a time until you reach desired consistency. Let boil for at least 1 minute.

Add steak to reheat and mix well.

If you've got leftover steak, all you have to do is a quick reheat. You don't want to overcook it. And if it's seasoned steak, be careful not to over-season it, too. This is a simple, quick stir-fry that makes it easy to dress up leftover steak.

Sloppy Joe Nachos

Serves 4

1 bag tortilla chips
½ red bell pepper, julienned
1 cup sliced fresh mushrooms
2 cups shredded sharp cheddar cheese
1 quart sloppy joe mixture
Jalapeño peppers, sliced

Garnish
Chopped cilantro

Preheat oven to 350°F. Place tortilla chips in a casserole dish. Top with red bell peppers, mushrooms, and cheese. Spoon sloppy joe mixture on top. Repeat layer. Finish final layer with jalapeño peppers, red bell peppers, and cheese. Bake for 10 minutes. Garnish with cilantro.

If you've got leftover sloppy joe but no buns, how about nachos? I like to layer my nachos, like lasagna, and you can add whatever you have on hand. Try adding vegetables and add lots of cheese. It's all about having fun in the kitchen.

MIKEY MONIS

This hearty hamburger steak frittata redefines breakfast goals. Bursting with bold flavors and wholesome goodness, this fusion creation is guaranteed to leave you craving more. We were lucky to have homemade hamburger steak made by Mikey's dad.

Hamburger Steak Frittata

Serves 4

½ red onion, diced
1 (15-ounce) can corn
Leftover Salisbury steak with gravy
Shredded cheese
8 eggs

Chop the Salisbury steak into small cubes. Keep gravy separate.

In a medium pan, sauté diced onions and 1 can of corn. Once the vegetables are heated up, add Salisbury steak, without the gravy, to the pan. When everything is nicely cooked, add in the gravy from the Salisbury steak; mix well so that nothing burns.

While that is cooking, whisk eggs then add to the pan. Let the eggs cook along with the rest of the ingredients, do not stir. Top frittata with shredded cheese and turn the stove to low-medium. Cover the pan for 10 minutes to let the ingredients steam and cook together. After 10 minutes, everything should be all cooked together like a pancake. If the eggs and cheese are still a little undercooked, cover the pan for a few more minutes to cook until it turns into a pancake. Once the frittata pancake is cooked, transfer to a nice plate and serve.

ERAN, BARBEA AND ZEZA GANOT

Wai'alae Beef Stew Sliders

Serves 2

2 cups leftover beef stew
2 bread rolls
1 teaspoon olive oil
1 tablespoon Kraft Shredded Mild Cheddar Cheese

Preheat oven to 325°F.

In a small saucepan, reheat beef stew. Cut rolls in half, place in a casserole dish and drizzle with olive oil. Spoon beef stew on each roll and top with cheddar cheese. Bake for 10 to 15 minutes.

Got some leftover beef stew but want to serve it in a new way? Try open-faced sliders. All you're doing is reheating, but presenting it in a whole new way so your family won't say, "Aw, stew again?"

Ube Corn Dogs

Serves 4 to 8

1 package Da Kine Hawaiian Ube Coconut Pancake Mix
2 tablespoons cornmeal
8 wooden sticks
8 hot dogs
8 mozzarella cheese slices
Cooking oil

Prepare pancake mix as directed and add cornmeal. Set aside.

Insert skewers into hot dogs. Slice hot dog lengthwise and stuff with cheese slice. Dip the hot dogs fully into pancake batter mixture. Deep fry for 3 to 4 minutes until golden brown.

This is an unbelievable pancake batter—you can smell the ube in the mix. People in Hawai'i are familiar with ube, a purple yam that's often used in desserts because of its sweet, nutty flavor. Adding cornmeal to the batter gives it a little crunch.

Kebabs with Asian Glaze

Serves 4

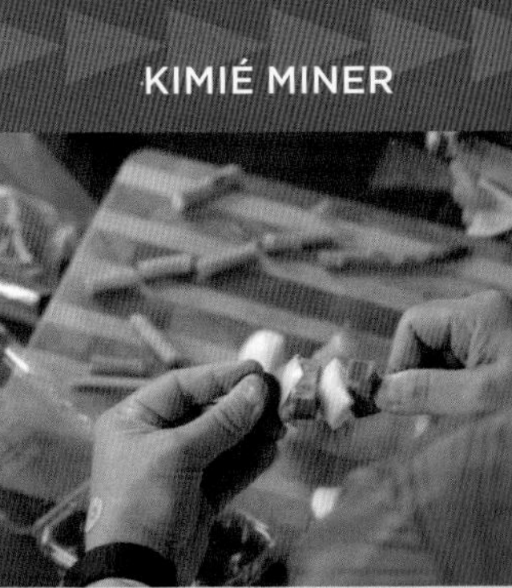

These little kebabs are a fun finger food for kids. Don't be afraid to experiment with your sauces and jellies. Just think about how you're balancing out flavors—we've got the tang of the barbecue sauce and the sweetness of the jelly and I reduced it down to make it more like a glaze than a sauce.

1 Portuguese sausage, cut into 1-inch pieces
½ onion, cut into wedges
1 dozen cherry tomatoes
4 asparagus spears, sliced into even pieces
¼ cup Halm's Hawaiian Bar-B-Que Sauce
½ cup liliko'i jelly

Alternately thread sausage, onions, cherry tomatoes, and asparagus pieces onto skewers.

Pan fry skewers until the vegetables are tender and the sausage is cooked through. Remove from heat.

In a small saucepan, combine barbecue sauce and liliko'i jelly. Cook until well-combined. Brush glaze evenly over each skewer and serve warm.

You may think you can't do anything with just a cup of leftover meat jun. But you can. Expand it by adding ingredients you have on hand and make lettuce wraps.

Taegu Lettuce Wraps

Serves 2 to 4

1 head lettuce
1 cup chopped taegu
1 tablespoon chopped onions
2 tablespoons chopped tomatoes
1½ tablespoons meat jun sauce
½ tablespoon taegu sauce
1 cup julienned meat jun
1 small tomato, sliced
Cilantro leaves for garnish

Break off lettuce leaves and keep whole. Wash lettuce thoroughly, pat dry, and set aside.

In a medium bowl, combine taegu, onions, tomatoes, and sauces. Mix well. Spoon mixture into the center of a lettuce leaf and top with a slice of meat jun. Garnish with a tomato slice and cilantro leaves.

Stuffed Winter Melon

Serves 4

2 (14.5-ounce) cans chicken stock, divided use
1 winter melon, seeded and cored (peel and dice the ends)
6 cloves garlic, chopped
1 teaspoon chopped ginger
1½ cups chopped shiitake mushrooms
1 pound smoked meat, cubed
1 carrot, cubed

Garnish
Sliced green onions

Heat 1 can of chicken stock in a large pressure cooker.

Cut ends of the winter melon to create a flat surface and set ends aside. Core the inside of the winter melon and remove the seeds. Place cored melon inside the pot.

Peel and dice the winter melon ends and set aside. Place garlic, ginger, shiitake mushrooms, smoked meat, carrots, and diced winter melon ends into the center of the cored winter melon all the way to the top. Add the second can of chicken stock; pour some inside the winter melon and the rest around the outside. Seal pot and cook for 15 to 20 minutes.

Carefully remove the stuffed winter melon and place in a large bowl. Pour remaining broth in the pressure cooker around the base of the melon. Garnish the top with sliced green onions.

Winter melons are so big and hearty, you can use them as a cooking vessel. Cooking it in a pressure cooker saves lots of time. Don't be afraid to fill the inside of the melon all the way to the top. It won't overflow. The filling will all drop down during the cooking process.

If you think about it, cooking really comes down to experimentation and improvisation. Sure, there are some hard and fast recipes that you want to follow, but they got that way after trial and error. This hash was named by Billy Souza because he got into the spirit of creating something new and different.

Hakimo Road Hash

Serves 4

2 boiled potatoes, mashed
½ cup kālua smoked ham
½ cup kālua corned beef
½ cup kālua pork
1 small onion, minced
¼ cup chopped green onions
2 tablespoons garlic chives
2 tablespoons poi
Panko
Cooking oil

Dipping Sauce
2 tablespoons mayonnaise
1 tablespoon Kewpie mayonnaise
1 tablespoon Aloha Shoyu Soy Sauce

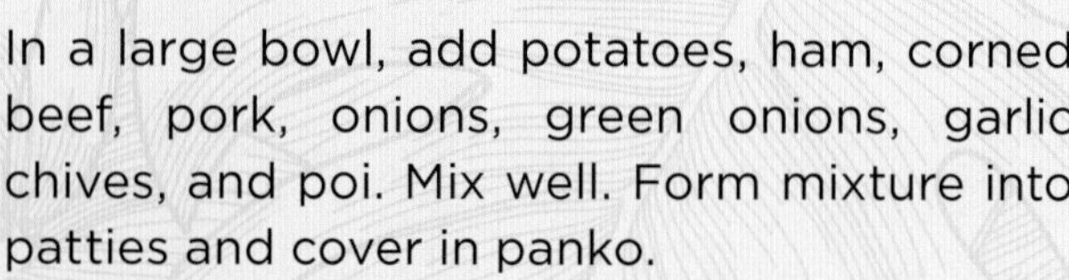

In a large bowl, add potatoes, ham, corned beef, pork, onions, green onions, garlic chives, and poi. Mix well. Form mixture into patties and cover in panko.

In a skillet, heat cooking oil over medium heat. Fry patties for 5 minutes. Flip patties over and cook another 5 minutes or until golden brown.

Mix Dipping Sauce ingredients together in a small bowl until well-combined, drizzle over patties and serve.

DR. CHRISTOPHER AND ROBYN LYNCH

Country Beef Stew

Serves 4

1 pound beef, cut into 1-inch cubes
1 tablespoon minced onion
1 tablespoon minced garlic
2 cups beef stock
2 celery stalks, chopped
12 baby carrots
5 red potatoes, quartered
½ (15-ounce) can tomato sauce
1 tablespoon water to thin tomato sauce
½ kabocha, cut into 1-inch cubes

Brown beef over medium-high heat. Add onions and garlic, sauté until tender. Cook for 20 to 30 minutes. Add beef stock and braise on medium-high on stove top for 1 to 1-1/2 hours. Once meat has softened, add the remaining vegetables. Cook for 35 minutes until vegetables are tender.

This is a hearty stew, and with the kabocha and potatoes in there, you don't have to serve it with rice or an extra starch. Kabocha is a Japanese winter squash that has a sweet flavor and a texture similar to pumpkin and sweet potato combined.

LE CREUSET

Papa's Beef Stew

Serves 4

3 tablespoons oil
2 pounds chuck roast, cut into cubes
1 cup minced onions
1 cup minced celery
2 tablespoons minced garlic
2½ cups chicken stock
2½ cups beef stock
Salt and pepper, to taste
2 medium carrots, cut into stew chunks
4 stalks of celery, cut into stew chunks
2 medium onions, cut into stew chunks
4 medium potatoes or baby assorted potatoes, cut into stew chunks
1 cup flour
1 cup canola oil

This is a recipe passed down to me from my dad. Every time I cook it, wherever I am, all over the world, I tell them this is a Hawaiian beef stew. My dad's secret was to cook the onions and celery with the beef, not separate. It flavors the beef and caramelizes the whole pan. This recipe was in one of my first cookbooks. It's a classic, Hawaiian stew.

In a large pot, heat oil. Add beef, onions, and celery then sauté for about 15 to 20 minutes until the liquid evaporates. Add garlic, chicken stock, and beef stock and stir well. Add salt and pepper to taste. Bring to a boil and let simmer for 45 minutes until the meat is tender. Add carrots, celery, onions, and potatoes and cook for 45 more minutes until veggies are soft.

To make a *roux,* combine 1 cup flour and 1 cup canola oil and mix well. Heat in the microwave for 2 minutes. Stir until mixture is well-combined.

Slowly add *roux* mixture to the stew until you have the consistency you want. Serve with hot rice or poi and enjoy!

MAX UNGER

The secret to making a good stew is to first brown the beef and vegetables to get a nice sear. Go high heat, blast it, and what we want to do is deglaze the pot. You'll see some nice golden brown on the bottom of the pot. Let all the liquid that comes out of the beef and onions cook down before you add the water. When you add the water, it starts to deglaze and that's where all the flavor comes from. Dutch ovens are perfect for making stews.

Lūʻau Beef Stew

Serves 4

3 pounds beef, cubed
2 cloves garlic, chopped
1 onion, chopped
2 quarts water
2 cups cooked lūʻau leaves
Salt, to taste

In a large pot, brown meat and garlic over medium-high heat. Add onions and cook for several minutes. Add water and bring to a boil. Lower heat and cook until the meat is tender (approximately 60 to 90 minutes). Add lūʻau leaves and salt. Stir well and cook for 15 additional minutes.

Korean Beef Stew

Serves 4

2 tablespoons olive oil
2 pounds stew beef, cut into 1-inch cubes
16 ounces beef stock
½ cup minced onions
1 cup chopped celery, divided use
1 cup roughly chopped cilantro
2 medium onions, chopped
1½ cups quartered mushrooms
1½ cups halved baby carrots
1 teaspoon minced garlic
Salt and pepper, to taste
1 packet Hawaiian Pride Kim Chee Fried Rice Sauce

Garnish
Kim Chee
Chopped cilantro

Heat olive oil in a stew pot over medium-high heat. Add beef and brown evenly. Add beef stock, minced onions, ½ cup celery, and cilantro. Bring to a boil. Cover and cook for 25 minutes. Add the remaining vegetables (½ cup celery, chopped onions, mushrooms, carrots, garlic), salt and pepper, and fried rice sauce and cook for an additional 20 minutes.

Garnish with kim chee and cilantro. Serve hot.

The key to a good stew is to sear the meat which will result in some nice caramelizing; stir up all that flavor with the *mirepoix* of onions, celery, and carrots. The Kim Chee Fried Rice Sauce really gives this a great flavor and kicks this stew up a notch.

This is a hearty Irish stew and the Guinness stout gives the lamb a deep, rich flavor. There's a lot of things you can do with the stew if you have leftovers. You can make a shepherd's pie—put the stew in a baking dish, layer mashed potatoes on top, and bake it. Or you could make a pot pie and bake a crust over the stew. Or you can serve it on rice, like what most people would do in Hawai'i.

Guinness Lamb Stew

Serves 4 to 6

2 tablespoons olive oil
1 boneless leg of lamb, cut into 2-inch pieces
½ package bacon, sliced
2 tablespoons minced garlic
1 onion, chopped
4 stalks celery, cut into ½-inch pieces
¾ cup sweet peppers, cut into ½-inch pieces
4 carrots, cut into ½-inch pieces
1 small bag assorted round potatoes, halved
4 sprigs fresh thyme
3 cans Guinness beer
2 cups beef stock
1 bay leaf
Salt and pepper, to taste
½ cup butter
½ cup flour
1 bag frozen peas
1 cup pearl onions, drained

Heat olive oil in a Dutch oven over high heat. Add lamb, bacon, and garlic. Cook for 2 to 3 minutes. Add onions, celery, sweet peppers, carrots, potatoes, and thyme. Braise and allow lamb to brown well. Add Guinness beer, beef stock, bay leaf, salt, and pepper. Cover and cook for 15 to 20 minutes.

To make the *roux,* use equal parts butter and flour. In a saucepan, melt butter over medium-high heat. Slowly whisk in flour until well-combined. To thicken stew, add *roux* and mix well. Remove thyme sprigs. Add peas and pearl onions. Continue to cook until vegetables are tender, about 35 minutes. Serve hot with Crusty Irish Soda Bread, page 44.

Fresh Corned Beef with 'Ulu and Taro

Serves 4

Corned beef and cabbage is a classic Irish dish. We decided to make this island-style with 'ulu and taro. What makes this recipe easy is using the already prepared 'ulu that's available in stores across the state by the Hawai'i 'Ulu Coop. The 'ulu is already peeled and cubed and ready to cook with.

- **2 to 3 pounds fresh corned beef with spice packet**
- **2 onions, quartered**
- **3 carrots, cut into 1-inch pieces**
- **1 (12-ounce) bag frozen 'ulu**
- **1 (12-ounce) bag frozen taro**
- **1 head cabbage, cut into wedges**
- **Salt and pepper, to taste**

In a large pot, place corned beef, spice packet, and enough water to cover ingredients. Bring to a boil. Reduce heat and simmer until corned beef is tender. Add vegetables and cook for 45 to 60 minutes.

Once cooked, slice corned beef and arrange on a serving platter with the vegetables. Add some hot broth and enjoy.

Tripe Stew

Serves 4

6 cups water for parboiling
1 pound tripe
1 (8-ounce) can tomato sauce
4 ounces water for stew
½ medium onion, sliced
½ bell pepper, sliced
1 stalk celery, julienned
3 cloves garlic, minced
1 small carrot, julienned
Salt and pepper, to taste

Bring water to a boil in a pot. Parboil tripe under tender then slice into strips.

In a large skillet, add tripe slices, tomato sauce, water, onions, bell pepper, celery, garlic, and carrots. Stir, cover, and cook until tender. Season with salt and pepper to taste. Pour stew into a large bowl and serve hot.

Tripe is the lining of beef, hog, or sheep stomach, but in grocery stores, you'll usually find tripe from beef. It's tough and requires long cooking for tenderness.
For this stew, we parboil it first to help quicken the softening process. Slicing it small also helps with the cooking process. You could also add potatoes to this stew to make it heartier.

Instant Pot Spicy Braised Short Ribs

Serves 4

10 pieces of short rib
Salty Wahine Hot Lava Seasoning, to taste
1 tablespoon oil
2 cloves garlic, minced
1 onion, diced
5 mini yellow bell peppers, sliced
½ cup Aloha Shoyu Kalbi Sauce
¼ teaspoon cumin
½ teaspoon cayenne

Coat each side of the short ribs with seasoning and press the seasoning into the meat. Once the short ribs are evenly coated with seasoning, let them rest so the seasoning melts into the meat. After you have rested the short ribs for about 15 minutes it's time to sear.

Add oil to a fry pan and heat stove to medium-high. Once frying pan is heated, sear all sides of the short rib until it has a nice brown color. Remove short ribs from the pan and let it rest on the side. With the excess oil from the pan, sauté garlic, onions, and yellow peppers. Once all ingredients are sautéed add in kalbi sauce, cumin, and cayenne to wake it all up. When everything is nice and heated on the stove, add in 1/4 cup of water to dilute the sauce. Add short rib and sautéed vegetables with the sauce mixture into the instant pot on medium-high. Once all ingredients are added to the pot let the short ribs cook for 35 minutes or until soft. After the short ribs are cooked shred the meat and eat as you desire.

The Salty Wahine seasoning gives these ribs a spicy, smoky flavor. Always bring your meat to room temperature before cooking and allow the seasoning to melt into the meat. Caramelizing is an important step before adding the meat to the instant pot. On the show, we served the rib meat in tacos, but you can serve it with mashed potatoes, rice, or whatever.

Short Rib Stew

Serves 4

2 pounds short ribs
1 tablespoon Salty Wahine Red Hawaiian Sea Salt and Rainbow Peppercorn
1 teaspoon Salty Wahine Starfruit Lemon Pepper
1 tablespoon olive oil
3 tablespoons Aloha Shoyu Gluten-Free Soy Sauce, divided use
1 teaspoon flour
1 large onion, chopped
2 stalks celery, chopped
2 carrots, chopped
1 box organic chicken bone broth
1 (15-ounce) can tomato sauce
2 tablespoons Aloha Bites Cacao Jelly
1 cup red wine

Place short ribs in a medium-sized bowl. Start by seasoning the short ribs. Add Salty Wahine seasonings, olive oil, and 1 tablespoon soy sauce. Gently massage the seasonings into the ribs to marinate the meat. After you massage the seasoning into the short ribs, lightly coat with flour and massage the short ribs until everything is coated evenly.

In Hawai'i we're lucky to have a variety of unique seasonings like the Starfruit Lemon Pepper seasoning from local Kaua'i company Salty Wahine. Starfruit may not be the first thing you think of when you think ribs, but its subtle sweet-sour flavor combined with the lemon really elevate these ribs into a memorable dish.

While the short ribs marinate, start prepping the *mirepoix.* Chop up onions, celery, and carrots to create the *mirepoix.*

Brown the short ribs in a large pan, then add in the *mirepoix* and sauté. Once everything is slightly cooked, transfer to a crock pot. Pour in chicken bone broth until it covers all the meat. Then add tomato sauce, 2 tablespoons of soy sauce, cacao jelly, and red wine to the crock pot. Give the pot a little stir then close it up and let it cook on high for 2 hours. After 2 hours, check to see if the meat is nice and tender. If not close it up and cook until your desired texture.

Island-Style Kalbi Ribs

Serves 4 to 6

4 to 5 pounds boneless short ribs
2 Asian pears (can substitute with apples), finely grated
1 clove garlic, finely minced
1 onion, grated
2 cups sliced green onions, divided use
1 tablespoon grated ginger
1 cup Aloha Shoyu Soy Sauce
3 cups brown sugar
½ cup sesame oil
3 tablespoons gochugaru
4 tablespoons sesame seeds, divided use

In a large bowl, soak short ribs in cold water for 45 minutes. Remove meat and dab dry.

In another large bowl, combine Asian pears, garlic, onions, 1 cup green onions, and ginger. Add soy sauce, brown sugar, sesame oil, gochugaru and 3 tablespoons sesame seeds. Add short ribs; mix well and cover ribs. Marinate for 4 hours.

Heat a grill to medium-hot. Grill short ribs to desired doneness. Garnish with 1 cup of green onions and 1 tablespoon sesame seeds.

Kalbi ribs are so tasty and easy to barbecue. This recipe shows you how to make the kalbi sauce from scratch. And, it may sound weird, but if you soak the meat in water after slicing it, the water will extract the blood and open up the pores so the meat will soak up the marinade more.

Umu Cooked Prime Rib

Serves 4 to 6

4 to 5 ti leaves
1 prime rib, whole
1 bottle oyster sauce
1 to 1½ cups prime rib seasoning (can substitute with garlic salt or Hawaiian salt)

Line a large foil baking pan with 2 ti leaves. Place prime rib fat side up in the pan, slather with oyster sauce and coat with seasoning on both sides. Cover prime rib with ti leaves then cover pan with tin foil. Cook in a preheated umu for 3 hours.

To make this in the oven, start by cooking the prime rib at 500°F for 15 minutes and then lower the oven temperature to 325°F and cook for 10 to 12 minutes per pound for rare; 13 to 14 minutes per pound for medium rare; 14 to 15 minutes per pound for medium-well.

NOTE: *A Samoan umu is like the Hawaiian imu except it's an above-ground, not underground, oven heated with hot volcanic stones. Food is wrapped in banana leaves or coconut fronds and placed on top of the stones. More banana leaves cover the top to seal the oven.*

You're gonna get your hands dirty preparing this one. Slather the oyster sauce all over the prime rib, lomi it in there. You may not have considered using oyster sauce to season prime rib, but if you think about it, it's a great marinade—it's got everything in there. It has the sugar that helps to brown it and gives it a nice caramel color. Place the prime rib fat side up so the fat will melt down into the meat, flavoring it and keeping it juicy. We made this prime rib in a Samoan umu with Tanoai Reed. Of course, you can make this in your oven with the same seasoning, no problem. You can even include the ti leaves.

Kilawin-Style Lānaʻi Venison

Serves 4

2½ tablespoons olive oil
1 pound Lānaʻi venison backstrap
3 tablespoons Aloha Shoyu Tamari
1 tablespoon minced garlic
1 tablespoon Lānaʻi salt
½ teaspoon black pepper
½ cup lime juice
3 tablespoons minced ginger
½ cup sliced green onion bottoms
1 white onion, sliced
2 Sensei Farms tomatoes, cut into wedges

Garnish
Wasabi leaves

Rub oil all over venison, both sides. Create a marinade by combining tamari, garlic, salt, and pepper. Place the venison fillets in a dish with the marinade and marinate for 10 to 15 minutes.

Grill venison fillets for 3 to 4 minutes per side (rare). Rest for 5 minutes then slice into thin pieces. Place sliced venison in a large mixing bowl. Add lime juice, ginger, green onions, white onions, and tomatoes. Mix well. Serve on wasabi leaves.

Kilawin was my favorite dish growing up on the north shore. The venison in this dish is prepared rare and sliced thin. We add freshly squeezed Meyer's lime juice to help the cooking process after grilling, like a ceviche. And the salt comes from the tamari.

Moloka'i Venison Stir-Fry

Serves 4

1 pound venison, sliced
1 teaspoon cornstarch
½ teaspoon sesame oil
½ medium onion (½ chopped and ½ sliced), divided use
½ shot whiskey
1 tablespoon olive oil
1 stalk lemongrass (cut into 3 [1-inch] pieces and smashed)
2 medium tomatoes, quartered and chopped
½ cup water
1 packet tomato seasoning

Garnish
Sliced green onions

The lemongrass is so aromatic and gives the venison such a nice flavor. You know, there's a reason stir-frying is so popular in Hawai'i. It's because it's quick and easy. Everyone is so busy working, commuting, taking care of family. Stir-frying is versatile because you can throw whatever you have on hand in there. As long as you have some seasoning, some nice sauces, and a protein, you're good to go.

In a large mixing bowl, combine venison, cornstarch, sesame oil, chopped onions, and whiskey. Mix well and set aside.

In a wok, heat olive oil over medium-high heat. Add lemongrass and venison mixture. Stir-fry for 4 to 5 minutes. Pour venison back into the mixing bowl and reserve. In the same wok, stir-fry sliced onions and tomatoes. Add water and tomato seasoning. Once the veggies are done, add the venison mixture back into the wok and mix well.

Place on a serving dish, garnish with green onions and serve.

Venison Tartare

Serves 4

8 ounces venison loin, finely chopped
1 tablespoon grated fresh ginger
1 tablespoon chopped green onions
1½ tablespoons olive oil
Salt, to taste
Juice of ½ lime
Juice of ½ tangerine
Butter
Bread slices

In a bowl, add venison, ginger, green onions, olive oil, salt, and citrus juices and mix well.

In a skillet, melt butter and toast bread slices until crispy. Spoon tartare onto toasted bread and enjoy.

The venison we prepared with Kelly Slater was harvested from Moloka'i. When you think about it, the deer doesn't eat anything but grass. Because we had such high-quality, fresh meat, we decided to serve it raw. When you add the citrus to help cook it a little, you'll see the color of the venison change a little.

Pan-Seared Venison with Traditional Chimichurri

Serves 4

1½ teaspoons olive oil
1 pound venison loin, cut into fillets
Salt and pepper, to taste

Chimichurri
¼ cup coarsely chopped parsley
1 tablespoon coarsely chopped cilantro
3 tablespoons red wine vinegar
4 cloves garlic, minced
2 tablespoons oregano leaves
2 teaspoons crushed red pepper
Salt and pepper, to taste
½ cup olive oil

In a large skillet, heat olive oil over medium-high heat. Season venison with salt and pepper. Cook fillets about 5 to 7 minutes per side. Remove from heat and let fillets rest.

In a small bowl, combine the parsley, cilantro, vinegar, garlic, oregano, and crushed red pepper. Season with salt and pepper. Pour olive oil over the mixture and mix well.

Cut venison into thin slices against the grain and serve with Chimichurri as a dipping sauce.

Pro-surfer Shane Dorian and his family shared some freshly harvested venison with us. Wild game meat has very little fat on it compared to the meat found in stores. And with wild game, you don't need a lot of seasoning. Simple salt is enough, and pepper if you want to add pepper. The key to pan searing the meat is to let it rest after searing. You don't want to overcook it, because wild game gets chewy if it's even slightly overcooked.

RAYMOND NOH

Teriyaki Venison with Noh Hula-Hula Sauce, Okra, and Tomatoes

Serves 2 to 4

Hula-Hula Sauce is bank and gives this venison a sweet gingery flavor. You can marinate the venison in the sauce before frying.

1 pound venison, sliced
¼ yellow onion, sliced
1 cup fresh okra, trimmed and chopped
6 grape tomatoes, halved
1 cup Noh Hula-Hula Sauce

Sear venison in a large skillet over high heat. Reduce heat to medium and add onions, okra, and tomatoes. Stir-fry for 2 minutes. Add Hula-Hula Sauce and allow to caramelize while stir-frying. Place on a platter and serve.

Kim Chee Fried Rice

Serves 4

2 tablespoons unsalted butter
½ medium onion, diced
1 cup diced Halm's Kim Chee
2 cloves garlic, minced
½ cup small diced Spam
2½ cups cooked rice
2 teaspoons cooking oil
2 eggs, beaten
½ cup chopped green onions (reserve 1 tablespoon for garnish)
1 teaspoon sesame oil
1 tablespoon Aloha Shoyu Soy Sauce
3 tablespoons of Hawaiian Pride Kimchee Fried Rice Sauce

Garnish
Mishima Nori Komi Furikake

In a skillet over medium-high heat, melt butter and sauté onions until slightly translucent. Add Halm's Kim Chee and garlic and cook for 2 to 3 minutes. Add Spam and cook for another 1 to 2 minutes. Add rice and mix well.

In a nonstick pan, heat vegetable oil over medium heat. Scramble the eggs until cooked. Remove from heat then combine with rice mixture in the original skillet. Add green onions, sesame oil, Aloha Shoyu Soy Sauce, and Hawaiian pride Kimchee Fried Rice Sauce. Mix well. Garnish with Mishima Nori Komi Furikake and serve.

Scan to watch Sam make this dish!

MARK AND BETSY SAWYER

Chow fun noodles are wide, flat noodles made of rice flour that soak up the flavor of whatever you can think to add. It's kind of like "summah" fun because you can add summa this, summa that. This chow fun recipe is a good way to use up those last servings of protein like cashew chicken or teri beef.

Chow Fun

Serves 2 to 4

1 tablespoon oil
1 carrot, julienned
1 head of broccoli, chopped
½ block of Spam, julienned
1 cup sliced (1-inch pieces) green beans
1 to 2 teaspoons soy sauce
2 (20-ounce) packages chow fun noodles
1 teaspoon sesame oil
1 bunch of green onions, sliced into 1-inch pieces
1 tablespoon sesame seeds
1 cup cooked cashew chicken
1 cup cooked and sliced teri beef

Garnish
2 crab legs, sliced
1 handful cilantro, chopped
1 tablespoon sesame seeds

Heat oil in a deep pan. Add carrots and broccoli. Stir occasionally. Mix in Spam and green beans. Cook until al dente. Drizzle soy sauce into pan. Add noodles. Stir to combine. Drizzle in sesame oil; add green onions and sesame seeds. Add cashew chicken and teri beef. Stir to combine. Once noodles are hot, remove from heat. Garnish with crab legs, cilantro, and sesame seeds.

NOTE: *Don't use too much soy sauce, because the Spam is already salty.*

DWIGHT AND TRESE OTANI

Kau Yuk

Serves 4 to 6

Kau Yuk is pork belly with taro and can be found in a lot of neighborhood Chinese restaurants throughout Hawaiʻi, often enjoyed during family celebrations. The red bean curd in this kau yuk is what gives it a red color. If you want a brown color kau yuk, use white bean curd. Using a pressure cooker makes this a really quick dish to make.

- 1 pork butt, cubed
- 1½ pounds pork belly, cubed
- 2 bunches cilantro, roughly chopped (reserve some leaves for garnish)
- ½ bottle red bean curd
- 3 tablespoons sugar
- 1 cup chicken broth
- 1 teaspoon Chinese five-spice powder
- 5 garlic cloves, peeled and smashed
- 1 tablespoon green onions

Place pork in a pressure cooker. Layer the chopped cilantro on the cubed pork.

In a mixing bowl, combine red bean curd, sugar, chicken broth, and Chinese five-spice powder. Mix well and pour over the layer of cilantro. Place garlic cloves on top. Cook in the pressure cooker for 30 minutes. Place in large bowl and garnish with green onions and cilantro.

MIKE AND SANDY IRISH

Kōloa Rum Kālua Pork
with Sweet Charlie Kim Chee Cabbage

Serves 4

2 tablespoons olive oil
24 ounces Keoki's Kālua Pork
3 tablespoons kim chee juice
1 ounce Kōloa Spiced Rum
1 quart Sweet Charlie's Kim Chee
½ bottle Halm's Pickled Onions

In a large skillet, heat olive oil over medium heat. Add kālua pork and heat through.

In a small bowl, mix kim chee juice and rum and add to kālua pork in skillet. Remove from heat. Add kim chee and mix well. Top with pickled onions and serve.

You may not realize that your jar of kim chee is packed in some delicious juices that you can use to create a whole new sauce. For this recipe, we're mixing the juice from a jar of Sweet Charlie's Kim Chee with the Kōloa Spiced Rum before adding it to the kālua pork.

BYL AND BURNI LEONARD

Pulled Pork on Rice Patty

Serves 2

2 tablespoons olive oil
2 cups cooked rice
½ teaspoon Aloha Shoyu Soy Sauce
½ bunch watercress
1 chicken thigh, shredded
1½ cups cooked pulled pork
½ cup water

Garnish
1 tablespoon green onions

In a large skillet, heat olive oil over medium-high heat. Firmly form 2 patties out of the leftover cooked rice and coat with soy sauce. Fry patties until each side is browned. Add watercress and cook until wilted.

In a separate pot, cook chicken and pulled pork with water. Place patties on a plate and place watercress around the patties. Pour chicken and pork mixture on top of the patties; garnish with green onions. Serve hot.

This is a fun way to use up leftover cooked rice. Form a patty and fry it in oil with soy sauce. The watercress adds a nice flavor to this dish. When watercress is cooked, it loses a bit of its peppery taste but leaves a distinctive vegetable flavor which is delicious in stir-fries.

MARK AND BETSY SAWYER

Have leftover pork and want to make something fast? Stir-fry is the way to go. Thinly slice the vegetables and meat, get the pan hot, and you'll have a delicious, satisfying dish in no time.

Hoisin Marinated Pork Stir-Fry

Serves 2 to 4

1 tablespoon coconut oil
4 cloves garlic, sliced
1 onion, sliced
4 stalks celery, sliced at an angle
5 mushrooms, julienned
Sriracha, to taste
½ cup sherry
4 heads baby bok choy, sliced lengthwise
1 carrot, julienned
1 to 2 pounds leftover hoisin-marinated garlic pork, cooked and sliced
Sesame oil

Heat skillet. Add coconut oil. Add garlic and onion to skillet; cook for a few minutes. Add celery and mushrooms to skillet; stir and cook for a few minutes. Add another drizzle of coconut oil, then add sriracha to taste. Stir. Drizzle sherry into skillet and add bok choy and carrots and heat until al dente. Add pork to skillet. Heat for about 3 minutes.

Finish with a light drizzle of sesame oil.

NOTE: *Because the pork is already cooked, add it in last, just to heat it up.*

Pork Belly Stir-Fry with Bok Choy and Long Beans

Serves 4

1 tablespoon olive oil
1 pound pork belly, sliced
1½ cups chopped long beans (1-inch pieces)
1 pound bok choy, chopped, separate steams and leaves
1 packet Hawaiian Pride Shoyu Chicken Sauce
½ tablespoon Halm's Hawaiian Bar-B-Que Sauce
½ teaspoon Aloha Shoyu Temari Soy Sauce

In a large skillet, heat olive oil over medium heat. Pan fry pork belly until browned. Drain excess oil. Add long beans and bok choy stems and stir-fry for 2 to 3 minutes. Add shoyu chicken sauce, barbecue sauce, temari soy sauce, and bok choy outer leaves. Stir-fry for 2 minutes until cooked through. Serve hot.

MIKE AND SANDY IRISH

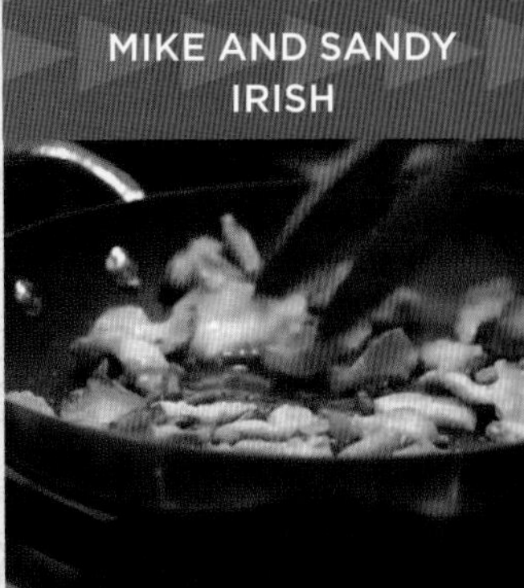

The sauce adds the magic to this dish. There's a little sweet and a little salty. Make sure you separate the bok choy stems and leaves. Stir-fry the stems first because they will take longer to soften up, and add the leaves last because they will cook quick.

Gon Lo Mein

Serves 4

3 tablespoons canola oil
1 pound chopped pork
2 tablespoons minced garlic
1 box chicken stock
2 medium carrots, julienned
4 stalks celery, julienned
2 medium onions, julienned
½ pound fresh sugar snap peas
2 tablespoons Aloha Shoyu Soy Sauce
2 tablespoons oyster sauce
1 bunch cilantro, reserve half for garnish
2 (12-ounce) packages chow mein noodles

In a large sauté pan, heat canola oil. Add pork and garlic and cook for 7 minutes. Add chicken stock and cook for about 3 minutes. Add carrots, celery, onions, sugar snap peas, soy sauce, oyster sauce, and half of the cilantro. Add chow mein noodles and cook for 3 to 4 minutes and mix well. Garnish with remaining cilantro and serve hot.

This is my dad's recipe. When I was growing up, people would come over to share their vegetables and next thing I knew, they would be walking out of the house with big pans of gon lo mein. I remember my dad saying the most important thing is cutting the vegetables all the same. Before making this dish, he'd have all the ingredients lined up, prepared and ready to go.

DESMOND AND TINA CURA

Making a quick chow fun is a great way to use up some leftover protein like chicken. Chow fun noodles are chewy wide rice noodles. When you add them to the vegetables, just fold them in gently so they don't break. The fina'denne sauce is a popular vinegar-soy condiment from Guam that adds a little heat to this dish. It's made with soy sauce, vinegar or fresh lemon juice, green onions, and chilis.

Chicken Chow Fun

Serves 2

2 tablespoons olive oil
½ medium red bell pepper, julienned
½ medium yellow bell pepper, julienned
½ medium green bell pepper, julienned
½ cup sliced onions
5 to 6 mushrooms, sliced
2 chicken breasts, cooked and sliced
4 tablespoons Aloha Shoyu Katsu Sauce
2 (7-ounce) packages chow fun noodles
3 tablespoons fina'denne sauce

Garnish
1 tablespoon chopped green onions
Sesame seeds

In a large skillet, heat olive oil. Add bell peppers, onions, and mushrooms and cook for 2 to 3 minutes over medium-high heat. Add chicken and katsu sauce and stir-fry for 2 to 3 minutes. Add chow fun noodles and fina'denne sauce. Mix well.

Garnish with sesame seeds and green onions.

"Konishiki-Fun" (Fried Kishimen Noodles)

Serves 4

2 (14-ounce) packages kishimen, cooked and drained
1 tablespoon olive oil
1 cup sliced ham
½ tablespoon Aloha Shoyu Soy Sauce
½ cup sliced shiro negi (white onions)
2 tablespoons mayonnaise
1 cooked hot dog
1 cooked turkey sausage
Black pepper, to taste
1 cup mixed greens

In a large pot, bring water to boil. Add kishimen and cook as directed. Place noodles in a strainer, shake to remove liquid, and set aside.

In a large skillet, heat olive oil over medium-high heat. Add kishimen, ham, soy sauce, and shiro negi and fry for 2 to 3 minutes. Slice hot dog and turkey sausage. Add mayonnaise, hot dog, turkey sausage, and pepper. Mix well over heat for a few minutes to heat through. Lastly, add mixed greens and toss well.

I had a blast cooking with sumo legend Konishiki. Saleva'a explained that in Japan, they cook with the white part of a green onion called shiro negi. It's called white onions. They slice it up and add it to most of their soups like miso soup. They don't eat the green part. Kishimen are the fatter noodles. You can add leftover proteins to a fried noodle dish like this, easy, and everything heats up in one pan.

Chicken Piccata

Serves 4

4 chicken breasts, boneless and skinless
1 cup flour (seasoned with salt and pepper)
2 to 3 tablespoons olive oil
1 cup chicken broth
3 to 4 tablespoons capers, drained
3 to 4 tablespoons lemon juice
3 to 4 tablespoons butter

This is a classic Chicken Piccata. Tender chicken breasts, delicately dredged and sautéed to golden perfection, then bathed in a luscious lemon-butter sauce with capers. Each bite is a symphony of flavors that will leave you swooning.

Preheat oven to 350°F.

Slice chicken breasts lengthwise to create thinner fillets. Using a mallet, pound each piece to ½-inch thickness. In a shallow dish, mix flour and season with salt and pepper. Dip the chicken to evenly coat both sides.

In a skillet, cook the chicken in olive oil until browned then place in a baking dish. In the same skillet, add broth, capers, lemon juice, and butter. Once creamy, pour the sauce over the chicken. Bake for 10 to 15 minutes or until chicken is cooked through.

MICAH SUDERMAN

Sommelier Micah Suderman suggested that a good wine pairing for Chicken Parmesan is a simple wine from Tuscany. San Giovesse is a classic grape that goes well with a dish that has tomato sauce and cheese. You can revive leftover spaghetti by putting it in a pot of salted boiled water for just a few minutes.

Chicken Parmesan

Serves 6

1 cup flour
Salt and pepper, to taste
1 tablespoon garlic powder
1 cup panko
1 cup grated Parmesan cheese
2 large eggs
6 chicken breasts, boneless and skinless
1 tablespoon cooking oil
1 jar pasta sauce
⅓ cup grated Parmesan cheese
1 cup shredded mozzarella cheese
6 cups cooked spaghetti noodles

Preheat oven to 375°F.

In a shallow dish, mix flour with salt, pepper, and garlic powder. In a separate shallow dish, combine panko and Parmesan cheese. In another shallow dish, whisk 2 large eggs. Pat the chicken dry. Dip both sides of the chicken into the flour, shaking off excess, then the egg, then the panko mixture. Evenly coat both sides. Fry in hot oil for 2 to 3 minutes on each side. Set aside to rest.

In a 13 x 9-inch baking dish, pour half the jar of sauce in an even layer and top with Parmesan cheese. Add chicken and evenly coat both sides of each breast with pasta sauce. Cover and bake for 30 minutes. Top with mozzarella cheese and continue to bake uncovered for 5 to 10 minutes or until mozzarella cheese is melted. Serve chicken and pasta sauce over a bed of cooked spaghetti.

Teriyaki Chicken Frittata

Serves 4 to 6

9 eggs, scrambled
1½ cups sliced mushrooms
1 tablespoon oil
½ onion, sliced
½ red bell pepper, sliced
3 pieces cooked bacon, cut into ½-inch pieces
2 pieces broccolini, sliced
12 asparagus spears, cut into 2-inch pieces
Salt and pepper, to taste
2 tablespoons julienned teriyaki chicken (cooked)
2 handfuls fresh spinach
½ cup shredded cheese
Sriracha, to taste

In a large bowl, scramble the eggs and stir in mushrooms. Set aside.

In a large skillet, heat oil and add onions, bell pepper, bacon, broccolini, and asparagus until tender. Season with salt and pepper. Add teriyaki chicken and stir well. Add egg mixture and cook over low to medium heat until eggs are almost set. Stir in spinach and top with shredded cheese. Drizzle with sriracha and serve.

If you've got a leftover protein like teriyaki chicken and a variety of vegetables, but you don't want to make another stir-fry, try a frittata. A frittata is similar to an omelet or quiche without the crust and is quick to make. They're also really easy to customize with whatever ingredients you have on hand.

Chicken Tinola

Serves 4

This classic Filipino soup is perfect for any occasion. In this recipe, we use tender chicken pieces with chayote, malunggay leaves, and ginger in a savory broth. It's a heartwarming dish that's both healthy and delicious. To really bring out the flavor, crush or smash the lemongrass stalks before sautéing.

1 tablespoon vegetable oil
½ medium onion, quartered
2 thumbs ginger, sliced
3 cloves garlic, minced
4 pieces lemongrass, smashed
1 whole chicken, cut and deboned
2 (32-ounce) boxes chicken stock
1 tablespoon chicken bouillon
2 tablespoons patis (fish sauce)
6 chayote, peeled and cut into 2-inch pieces
1 tomato, quartered
1 bunch long beans, cut into 2-inch pieces
½ cup malunggay leaves

In a large pot, heat oil over medium heat. Add onions, ginger, garlic, and lemongrass and sauté for 10 minutes. Add chicken and cook for 5 minutes. Add chicken stock, chicken bouillon, and patis. Bring to a boil and cook for 35 to 40 minutes or until chicken is cooked through. Add chayote, tomato, and long beans. Cook for 5 minutes. Lastly, add malunggay leaves and serve hot.

Chicken Tofu

Serves 2 to 4

1 teaspoon salt
½ cup chopped brussels sprouts
2 teaspoons olive oil
½ rotisserie chicken, shredded
1½ cups spinach
½ cup julienned onions
1 tablespoon minced garlic
1 teaspoon guava jelly
4 teaspoons Aloha Shoyu Somen Salad Dressing
1 (14-ounce) package firm tofu, sliced

Not every kitchen has a fully-stocked pantry at all times. If a recipe calls for a little sugar or honey to balance out the salt and you don't have either one, think outside the box. You can sweeten up a dish with jam or jelly, which will also add a nice kick of flavor.

Add salt to a pot of water and bring to a boil. Add brussels sprouts and boil for about five minutes. Remove brussels sprouts with a slotted spoon, and place into a bowl of ice water to stop cooking.

Heat olive oil in a medium-sized pan. Add chicken, spinach, onions, brussels sprouts, garlic, somen salad dressing, and guava jelly and sauté over medium heat.

Place tofu in a large, heat-resistant dish. Remove pan from heat and pour chicken mixture over tofu.

Aloha Shoyu Chicken

Serves 2

6 chicken drumsticks
1 cup water
1 tablespoon Aloha Shoyu Hawaiian Honey Teriyaki Glaze
¾ package Halm's Hawaiian Pride Shoyu Chicken sauce
1 cup sliced onions

Garnish
Celery hearts

In a skillet over medium-high heat, cook chicken drumsticks in water, teriyaki glaze, and chicken sauce. Add onions and bring to a boil. Cook until tender and sauce thickens. Place chicken on a serving platter and pour sauce over chicken. Garnish with celery hearts.

The sauces are key to this flavorful chicken. Keep a variety of sauces on hand so you can whip up dishes like this that don't require a lot of prep work.

You'll find something similar to this dish–not like what we did with leftovers, though—in any major restaurant in Hong Kong. But the idea is the same with the cake noodles and chicken. Again, you can come up with new ways to present your leftovers and when you don't have a lot, add what you've got in the kitchen.

Orange Chicken and Edamame Cake Noodle

Serves 4

2 (6-ounce) packages yakisoba noodles
2 tablespoons olive oil, divided use
½ yellow onion, sliced
2 cups leftover orange chicken
½ cup edamame
2 tablespoons Special Dressing (page 31)

Place yakisoba noodles in a colander and rinse under hot water. Shake to dry. In a skillet, heat 1 tablespoon olive oil over medium-high heat and fry noodles until crispy. Cut noodles into quarters and place on a serving dish.

In the skillet, heat 1 tablespoon olive oil and sauté onions until translucent. Add orange chicken and edamame. Add Special Dressing and mix well. Pour mixture over noodles and serve.

Mochiko Chicken Wrapped in Nori

Serves4

1 pound chicken breasts, boneless and skinless
½ cup mochiko flour
½ cup corn starch
2 tablespoons minced garlic
½ teaspoon minced ginger
2 tablespoons chopped green onions
½ cup Aloha Shoyu Soy Sauce
5 tablespoons sugar
1 tablespoon gochujang
1 egg
6 nori sheets, cut into 4-inch wide strips
Cooking oil

This mochiko chicken recipe is a little different. We added some heat with the gochujang and we wrapped pieces of chicken in nori before frying. This makes it a fun finger food or pūpū that you can share at a potluck or feed the kids after a long day at work.

Slice chicken breasts into strips and set aside.

In a bowl, add the rest of the ingredients and mix well. Add chicken and mix until well-coated. Spoon marinated chicken onto nori strips and roll tightly. Deep fry until chicken is cooked through and crispy.

LEROY AND TAMMY ABIRACHED

Chicken Yakitori with Creamy Rice and Bean Sprouts

Serves 4

½ tablespoon brown sugar
1 tablespoon Aloha Shoyu Soy Sauce
2 pounds chicken, sliced
1 tablespoon olive oil
2 tablespoons chopped green onions

In a medium dish, mix brown sugar and soy sauce. Add chicken slices and marinate for 15 minutes. Heat olive oil in a skillet over medium heat. Cook chicken for 5 to 7 minutes or until the chicken is cooked through. Garnish with green onions. Serve with Creamy Rice and Bean Sprouts.

If you have leftover rice but are tired of making fried rice, try a creamy rice. So simple with subtle flavors that can be paired with any protein.

Creamy Rice

2½ cups chicken stock
3 cups cooked rice
Salt and pepper, to taste
½ tablespoon Aloha Shoyu Soy Sauce
½ teaspoon sesame oil
½ cup chopped green onions
½ chopped cilantro

In a saucepan, heat chicken stock and fold in rice. Add salt, pepper, soy sauce, and sesame oil and stir (the consistency will be like thick oatmeal). Fold in green onions and cilantro.

Bean Sprouts

1 (10-ounce) package bean sprouts
½ tablespoon olive oil
1 tablespoon Aloha Shoyu Soy Sauce
1 tablespoon chopped cilantro
1 tablespoon green onions

In a sauté pan, cook bean sprouts in olive oil and soy sauce for 3 to 4 minutes or until bean sprouts are tender. Garnish with cilantro and green onions.

You don’t have to serve the same exact meal you served the night before. Get creative and improvise. Add some body and flavor to leftover chicken stew with some pasta and veggies. In a few easy steps, last night’s dinner can be reimagined into a whole new dish.

Braised Chicken Stew

Serves 4

5 cups leftover chicken curry stew
1 handful chopped cilantro
2 cups sliced (in half, lengthwise) baby carrots
1 handful chopped green onions
1 bell pepper, julienned
2 cups shell pasta, cooked
2 mushrooms, sliced lengthwise

Add chicken stew to large pot. Stir to heat. Once it starts simmering, add cilantro, carrots, green onions, and bell pepper. Stir to combine and simmer for a few more minutes to soften carrots.

Scoop cooked shell pasta into a large bowl.

Add mushrooms to pot. Once vegetables are tender, remove pot from heat and pour stew over pasta.

TIP: *Washing mushrooms water logs the mushroom. Instead, wipe the mushrooms with a dry cloth.*

Cauliflower "Fried Rice"

Serves 2

1 piece char siu chicken, sliced
1 tablespoon olive oil
1 strip of red bell pepper, diced
1 cup chopped onions
1 cup chopped fresh spinach
2½ cups cauliflower, finely grated and sautéed with olive oil, salt and pepper
1 teaspoon oyster sauce
1 teaspoon Aloha Shoyu Soy Sauce

Sauté chicken in olive oil for 2 minutes to reheat. Add red bell pepper, onions, and spinach. Cook for 3 minutes or until spinach is wilted. Add cauliflower, oyster sauce, and soy sauce. Mix well and serve.

Cauliflower rice is an excellent alternative to rice. To make it, you just chop up a head of cauliflower into large pieces (discard the leaves) and place in a food processor. Pulse until it has the texture of rice. It will kind of look like couscous.

SHANNON AND
MANDI SCOTT

With a little imagination, even the busiest families can try this twist on a classic dessert and turn their pizza party leftovers into a unique savory entrée.

Domino's Savory Bread Pudding

Serves 4

4 eggs
1 cup whole milk
½ teaspoon salt
½ teaspoon black pepper
Cooking spray
5 Domino's breadsticks, cubed
1 tray Domino's chicken Alfredo
4 Domino's hot wings
2 slices Spam, cubed
1 mushroom, sliced
½ onion, diced
2 handfuls of four-cheese mix

Preheat oven to 350°F. Whisk 4 eggs in a mixing bowl. Add milk, salt, and pepper to eggs and combine. Set aside.

Coat a 8 x 8-inch glass baking dish with cooking spray. Put cubed breadsticks into the baking dish. Put chicken Alfredo on top of the breadsticks and combine.

Pull meat off chicken wings and cube. Add chicken from hot wings, Spam, mushroom, and onion to the dish; combine. Top with four-cheese mix. Pour egg mixture evenly on top and top with a little sprinkling of cheese. Bake for about 30 minutes.

NOTE: *When cooking with leftovers, notice the flavor profile of the food you're using and notice what may already be seasoned. That way, you can be thoughtful about how much extra salt or other seasonings to add.*

Stuffed Bell Peppers with Curried Roasted Chicken Salad

Serves 2

If you have leftover roast chicken, chicken salad is the way to go. And even if you don't have that much chicken left, adding other ingredients like apples and onions stretches it out. Serve it inside sweet bell peppers, and you've got a tasty dish.

2 cups shredded roasted chicken
1 apple, peeled and diced
3 tablespoons chopped onions
1 tablespoon chopped green onions
⅓ packet curry seasoning
1¼ cups mayonnaise
½ teaspoon seasoning salt
2 sweet bell peppers, seeded and quartered

In a medium bowl, mix all ingredients except bell peppers. Scoop and pack mixture onto sweet pepper quarters. Arrange on a platter and serve.

DUSTIN AND TARA ALFORD

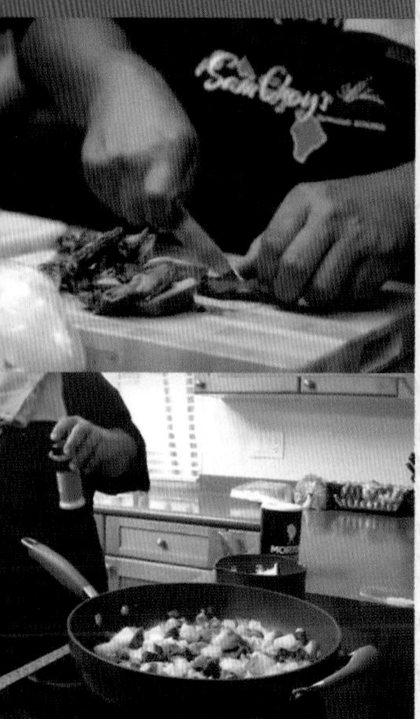

‘Uala, or sweet potatoes, were introduced to the islands from South America by Polynesian voyagers centuries ago and have been a staple of the Hawaiian diet. Not only is it good for you, but it’s delicious and versatile. Here we combine ‘uala with some leftover meats to make a hearty hash. The key to a good hash is to get a crispy crust.

Sweet Potato Hash

Serves 2 to 4

3 to 4 tablespoons olive oil
2 cups cooked and diced sweet potatoes
2 cups pulled chicken meat
2 cups cooked and diced beef
2 tablespoons minced garlic
1 medium red onion, diced
½ tablespoon salt
Black or white pepper, to taste
½ cup chopped green onions

In a thick sauté pan, reheat sweet potatoes in olive oil over medium-high heat for about 10 minutes. Add chicken, beef, garlic, and red onion. Season with salt and pepper. Cook for about 20 minutes then add green onions to finish.

Ground Turkey Patties

Serves 4

1 pound ground turkey
2 eggs
3 cloves garlic, minced
1 onion, diced
1½ teaspoons Spike Vegit Seasoning
1 teaspoon cornstarch
¼ cup chopped green onions
1 tablespoon milk
1 bunch cilantro, chopped
1 tablespoon Aloha Shoyu Low Sodium Soy Sauce
1 tablespoon olive oil

In a medium bowl add ground turkey, eggs, garlic, onion, Spike Vegit Seasoning, cornstarch, green onions, milk, cilantro, and soy sauce. Once all ingredients are added to the bowl, gently mix until everything is combined. Form burger-size patties out of the turkey mixture.

Heat olive oil in a medium size frying pan. Once oil is nice and hot, start frying the patties until they are nice and golden brown on each side. Serve with buns of your choice with all the fixings.

It's easy to breathe some life into simple ground turkey by just adding some eggs for moisture, garlic and onions for layers of flavor. The Spike Vegit Seasoning adds tons of flavor without adding extra sodium. It's a healthy alternative with low sodium, no sugar, no MSG, and is vegan. UH football linebacker coach, Chris Brown, said eating healthy was simply a way of life for him and a way to be a role model to his team by keeping himself in shape.

RUSSELL MARCHAN

If you've got some protein and want to serve something new, adobo it! You just need a base protein that you brown in oil then marinate and simmer in vinegar, salt, soy sauce, and garlic. The cooking method for Filipino adobo is indigenous to the Philippines, and vinegar is the most important ingredients in Filipino cuisine.

Turkey Tail Adobo

Serves 4

1 pound turkey tails, halved
1 finger ginger, sliced
4 cloves garlic, minced
½ cup green beans
3 bay leaves
1 teaspoon peppercorns
2 tablespoons vinegar
1 tablespoon Aloha Shoyu Soy Sauce
Water
Salt, to taste

In a large pot, braise turkey tails on medium-high heat and cook until browned. Lower heat and add ginger and garlic. Add green beans, bay leaves, peppercorns, vinegar, soy sauce, and water to cover. Bring to a light simmer and cook for 35 to 40 minutes until tails are tender. Season with salt. Pour onto a platter and serve hot.

Char Siu Turkey Sliders with Pickled Onions

Serves 4

1 tablespoon olive oil
1 pound leftover turkey, shredded
1 packet Hawaiian Pride Charsiu sauce
½ jar Halm's Kim Chee, chopped
3 tablespoons kim chee juice
2 tablespoons Best Foods Mayonnaise
8 Hawaiian Sweet Bread Rolls, halved
8 butter leaf lettuce leaves
2 tablespoons Halm's Pickled Onions

In a large skillet, heat olive oil and turkey over low heat. Add char siu sauce, kim chee, and kim chee juice. Toss well.

To assemble sliders, spread mayonnaise on sweet bread slices and place a lettuce leaf, turkey mixture, and pickled onions.

MIKE AND SANDY IRISH

When you think about your mom and your grandmother, you think how did they do it? How did they manage to feed the entire family day in and day out? They pre-made a whole bunch of stuff to use throughout the week, mixing and matching leftovers and creating new dishes. Char siu isn't just for pork. Transform leftover turkey with char siu sauce and if you have a jar of kim chee, you can use the juice as a stock—gives leftover turkey a nice extra kick.

ALMA & ALEJANDRO ALVARADO

‘Ahi Tostadas with Avocado Crema

Serves 4

4 tortillas
1 pound fresh ‘ahi, cut into 1-inch cubes
½ cup chopped green onions
½ cup chopped onion
1 medium tomato, chopped
1 jalapeño pepper, minced
3 tablespoons Aloha Shoyu Poke Sauce

Avocado Crema
1 ripe avocado
2 tablespoons sour cream
½ teaspoon minced garlic
½ cup fresh cilantro
Juice from ½ lime juice
Salt and pepper, to taste
Hot sauce, optional

Garnish
Fresh cilantro

Fry tortillas until crispy and set aside.

In a bowl, add ‘ahi, green onions, onions, tomatoes, jalapeño pepper, and poke sauce. Mix well and set aside.

Prepare Avocado Crema by mixing all ingredients until very well-combined. Scoop poke onto a tortilla, top with avocado crema and garnish with cilantro.

This is a fun and new way to eat poke—Mexican-style, in honor of restaurateur and chef Alejandro Alvarado and his mom, Alma. These crunchy delights are topped with succulent ‘ahi tuna, drizzled with a tangy avocado crema, and finished with a sprinkle of fresh cilantro and lemon.

This recipe is straightforward with only a few ingredients and even fewer instructions. The spicy sear of the fried poke and the fresh onion and cucumber has every bite bursting with flavor and contrasts nicely with the tofu.

Fried Poke

Serves 2

1 block firm tofu
½ onion, thinly julienned
¼ cucumber, julienned
1 cup spicy ʻahi poke
1 tablespoon oil
Sriracha, to taste
Soy sauce, to taste

Run tofu under cold water to rinse. Slice tofu into 1 x 1-inch segments, while keeping it in its original block form (don't separate segments), and place on a plate. Spread raw onions and cucumber over the tofu block.

Quickly sear poke in hot oil and remove from heat. Pour seared poke over tofu block, then pour any remaining fish oil in pan over the poke. Top with sriracha and soy sauce.

‘Ahi Tofu Patties

Serves 4

1 pound fresh ‘ahi meat, minced
1 tablespoon garlic
½ cup chopped onion
¼ cup chopped green onions
1 block firm tofu, excess water removed and crumbled
2 tablespoons Halm’s Kim Chee Poke Sauce
2 tablespoons Aloha Shoyu Poke Sauce
1 tablespoon sesame oil
Garlic salt, to taste
Oil

In a large bowl, add all ingredients and mix well. Roll the mixture into golf ball-sized balls.

In a skillet, heat oil over medium-high heat. Place the ‘ahi balls in the oil and let them brown a little before pressing them down into patties. Be very careful when pressing the ‘ahi balls into patties because there’s no binding in this recipe; no eggs, no bread-crumbs.

Pan fry the patties for 3 to 4 minutes per side or until browned.

If you want to make a dish that has the same flavors as ‘ahi poke, but isn’t poke, make patties. These little bite-sized patties can be served with a dip or in a lettuce wrap.

DARREN AU

Pan-Fried Fish with Kaua'i Sea Salt

Serves 3 to 4

3 whole fresh fish ('āweoweo and menpachi)
Kaua'i sea salt, to taste
3 tablespoons olive oil
Lemongrass leaves for plating

Garnish
Sliced green onions

Clean fish and season with Kaua'i sea salt. In a wok, heat olive oil over medium-high heat. Carefully place the fish in the wok and cook for about 3 minutes per side. Place fish on lemongrass leaves, garnish with green onions, and serve.

You can't beat freshly caught fish. It doesn't take much to make a delicious dish with fresh fish. It's a little seasoning and a quick cook and before you know it, dinner is on the table. In this recipe, we're cooking the whole fish in oil. Be very careful when adding it to the hot oil. Slide the fish in gently and step back because the salt on the fish will make the oil spit.

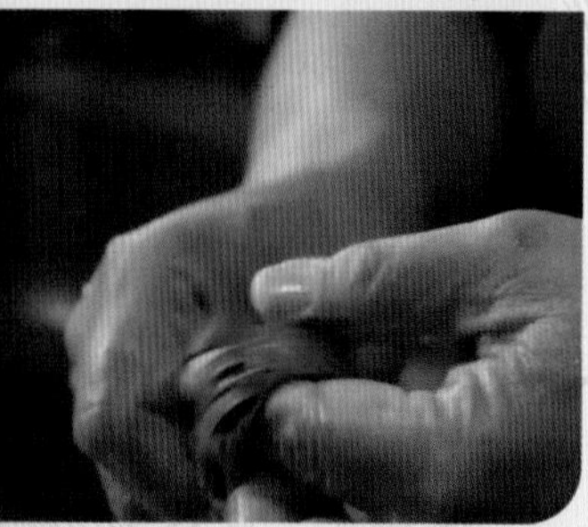

LEROY AND TAMMY ABIRACHED

Sautéed Mahimahi with 4,000 Island Dressing

Serves 4

1 tablespoon olive oil
2 pounds mahimahi fillets
Salt and pepper, to taste
½ teaspoon Aloha Shoyu Soy Sauce

In a large skillet, heat olive oil over medium-high heat. Season the fish fillets with salt and pepper. Cook fillets about 6 minutes per side until golden brown. Sprinkle soy sauce on top.

4,000 Island Dressing

4 tablespoons mayo
2 tablespoons ketchup
1 teaspoon Thousand Island dressing
½ teaspoon Aloha Shoyu Soy Sauce
½ teaspoon Dijon mustard
½ teaspoon pepperoncini juice
Pepper, to taste

In a small mixing bowl, combine all ingredients and mix well. Drizzle over fillets or use as a dipping sauce.

Mahimahi is a great fish to work with—just a center bone with lots of fillet—and when cooked right, it's tender, flaky, and full of flavor. When you're cooking fresh fish, make one side the hero side—the side that has a nice beautiful char. The other side you're cooking just to cook it. So when you plate the fish, the hero side is the side that's showing. Make sure you don't overcook the fish in the pan because it will keep cooking after you take it off the heat.

EGAN AND MARCIA INOUE

Jiu-jitsu and racquetball champion Egan Inoue and his wife Marcia are both very health conscious, and we had fun making carb-free meals at their home like this one. This is a really quick and easy recipe. Get some fresh salmon from the store and season it well. The salmon cooks fast. Using the same skillet you cooked the salmon in to stir-fry the mushrooms not only saves time, but allows the salmon flavor to infuse the mushrooms.

Salmon with Aloha Shoyu and Shiitake Mushrooms

Serves 6

6 small salmon fillets
Salt and pepper, to taste
2 tablespoons olive oil
2 tablespoons butter
1½ tablespoons teriyaki sauce
1 tablespoon sweet chili sauce
8 to 10 shiitake mushrooms, sliced
Aloha Shoyu Soy Sauce, to taste

Season salmon with salt and pepper. In a large skillet, heat olive oil over medium heat. Fry salmon skin side down for 5 to 7 minutes or until halfway done. Turn fillets over and cook for 1 to 2 minutes. Place fillets on a large serving platter.

Using the same skillet, melt butter. Add teriyaki sauce, sweet chili sauce, and mushrooms; stir-fry for 1 minute. Pour mixture onto salmon fillets. Top with soy sauce and serve.

Furikake Miso Salmon Tostadas

Serves 3

3 medium flour tortilla, fried (can be substituted with tortilla chips)
3 cups oven-roasted salmon
1 medium tomato, diced
3 tablespoons basil pesto oil
1 cup Kraft Real Mayo
Hot sauce (Tapatio or Sriracha), to taste
3 tablespoons Kraft Sweet & Thick BBQ sauce

Garnish
½ cup cilantro, chopped

In a skillet, fry flour tortillas. Place salmon, tomato, and basil oil on top of tortillas. Mix mayonnaise with hot sauce and Kraft BBQ sauce and drizzle over salmon. Garnish with cilantro.

If you don't want to eat the same dish you did the day before, make something new with your leftover salmon. These tostadas add some zing and turn the salmon into something new. When making the tostadas, be careful not to over fry the tortillas.

Lap Cheong Salmon

Serves 4

This is a local-style recipe for salmon. We've all done this with the lap cheong, the mayo, little soy, and this time we added some miso sauce. You can turn a large skillet into a modern day imu by using ti leaves. Cover the assembled salmon in the pan with ti leaves before covering with the lid which will give you a better steam–it helps steam the top leaving the bottom crisp. Just cut the ti leaves down to fit. Easy.

2 cups mayonnaise
2 tablespoons miso sauce
1 tablespoon Aloha Shoyu Soy Sauce
1 tablespoon minced garlic
2 cups cooked and thinly sliced lap cheong, divided use
2 pounds salmon fillet
Salt and pepper, to taste
½ red onion, sliced
2 tablespoons chopped green onions
2 tablespoons chopped cilantro
1 (3.5-ounce) package enoki mushrooms
2 ti leaves

In a bowl, add mayonnaise, miso sauce, soy sauce, garlic, and 1 cup lap cheong. Mix well.

Season salmon with salt and pepper and place in a large, deep skillet, skin side down, on medium-high heat. Spread the lap cheong mixture on the salmon fillet. Top with red onions, the remaining lap cheong, green onions, cilantro, and enoki mushrooms. Cover everything with 2 ti leaves, shiny side up; cover with lid and cook for about 3 to 4 minutes until salmon is cooked through.

Misoyaki Salmon

Serves 4

4 tablespoons Ohana Flavors Miso Sauce
1 tablespoon Ohana Flavors Shoyu Poke Sauce
1 pound fresh Verlasso salmon fillets
1 head Sensei Farms butterleaf lettuce

Garnish
2 tablespoons sliced green onions

Create a marinade by combining the Miso and Shoyu Poke Sauces. Place the salmon fillets in a baking dish and coat each fillet with the miso marinade. Marinate for 1 hour.

Grill salmon fillets for 4 minutes per side. Place on a bed of lettuce and garnish with green onions.

White miso sauce makes such a great marinade for salmon. Ideally, you could marinate the salmon for twenty-four hours. But if you're on a time-crunch, an hour is enough. The secret to grilling the salmon is to not touch it. And what I learned from expert grillers in Alaska, for salmon, you turn it just once.

We have to protect our oceans and make sure amazing fish like the freshly caught pāpio we were lucky to have is around for our kids to enjoy. Follow the rules and only keep the size of fish you're allowed. This is a simple recipe with a lot of flavor. Remember to score the fish so all that great seasoning gets into the meat.

Fresh Pāpio with Sautéed Vegetables

Serves 2

1 fresh pāpio, whole
1 tablespoon sea salt and 1 tablespoon garlic salt, mixed
1 teaspoon Salty Wahine Passion Fruit Chili Pepper seasoning
1 tablespoon cooking oil
2 tablespoons butter
4 cloves garlic, smashed
½ red onion, sliced
½ sweet red pepper, sliced
½ yellow bell pepper, sliced
12 mushrooms, sliced

Score pāpio and pat salt-garlic mix and chili pepper seasoning on both sides. Heat oil in a skillet and fry fish for 3 to 5 minutes until skin is crispy. Turn over and cook for another 3 to 4 minutes. Add butter and garlic. Baste the fish with melted butter.

Remove fish from skillet and place on a serving platter.

In the same skillet, add vegetables and sauté in butter garlic sauce until tender. Pour vegetables on fish and serve hot.

CHRIS, CLAIRE AND KA'IWA CHOY

Steamed Moi

Serves 2 to 4

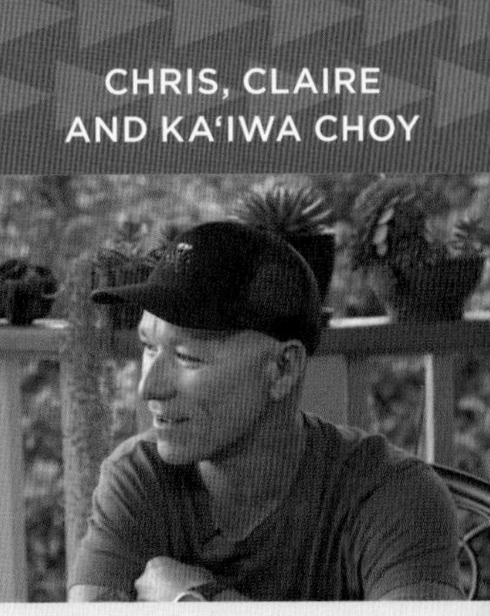

Scoring the fish allows it to cook evenly. And it also allows the seasoning and flavor to go through the fish. You know, moi is an ali'i fish. People tried to farm raise it, but I think this fish has to be cared for in the ocean.

1 whole moi
2 tablespoons chopped fresh ginger
White pepper, to taste
½ cup sliced green onions, divided use
4 links lap cheong, sliced
½ head cabbage, sliced
Garlic chili crunch, to taste
2 tablespoons seasoned oil with red pepper and garlic
½ cup peanut oil

Score fish and stuff with ginger. Season with pepper and top with green onions. Place in a large steamer lined with ti leaves and add a layer of lap cheong slices and ¼ cup green onions. Cook for 15 minutes. Carefully remove fish from steamer and place on a bed of cabbage. Top with garlic chili crunch. In a small saucepan, heat peanut oil and pour over whole fish.

NOTE: *Steaming the lap cheong with the fish gets some of the fat out, not all of it, but some, and it will add flavor to the fish. Lap cheong is the perfect complement to fish.*

Seafood Cioppino

Serves 4

- 1 tablespoon olive oil
- ½ tray button mushroom
- 8 cherry tomatoes, diced
- 1 large onion, chopped
- 5 garlic cloves, minced
- 1 red and 1 yellow bell pepper, sliced
- 1½ teaspoons dry basil seasoning
- 1 teaspoon Salty Wahine Island Volcano Seasoning
- 2 cups white wine, divided use
- 1 (15-ounce) can tomato sauce
- 1½ pounds shrimp
- 6 to 8 scallops
- 1 tablespoon Parks Brand Hawaiian Chili Pepper Water

In a medium sauté pan add olive oil to coat the pan. Once the pan and oil are nice and hot add mushrooms, cherry tomatoes, onions, garlic, and bell peppers into the pan and sauté. Season with dry basil and Salty Wahine Island Volcano Seasoning. When vegetables are soft, add 1 cup of white wine to cover the ingredients. Cook over medium heat until the alcohol is reduced. Once the alcohol is reduced and the ingredients have been simmering, add 1 can of tomato sauce. Stir all the ingredients together for a couple minutes then add in seafood and mix. Add remaining 1 cup of white wine until it covers the ingredients; let that reduce. Drizzle in the Chili Pepper Water; mix well and then it's ready to serve.

Enjoy this Cioppino with some bread or over hot rice.

Joking around with local comedian Island Magic Mike, I said the only place in the world where people would eat spaghetti and rice with mayonnaise on top, is Hawai'i. If you're in France or Italy, you would serve cioppino with a freshly baked baguette. Serve this cioppino with warm French bread or go ahead and serve it over rice, with a dollop of mayo, if you wish.

Shrimp and Spinach Stir-Fry

Serves 4

1 tablespoon olive oil
5 lap cheong sausages, sliced at an angle
2 cloves garlic, minced
3 carrots, sliced into sticks
½ medium onion, sliced
1 (8-ounce) package fresh spinach
12 to 16 shrimp, cleaned
1 tablespoon teriyaki sauce
½ teaspoon oyster sauce

In a wok, heat olive oil over medium-high heat. Add lap cheong and garlic and cook for 1 minute. Add carrots, onions, and spinach and cook until spinach begins to wilt. Add shrimp and stir-fry for 1 minute. Add teriyaki sauce and oyster sauce. Stir-fry ingredients until shrimp is cooked (about 3 to 4 minutes).

Lap cheong is great in a stir-fry. My dad taught me, when you cook, you always make everything look nice. Prep the vegetables and lap cheong in same-sized pieces. Stir-frying is so quick and easy, and you can add in pretty much whatever you have on hand. The only time-consuming part is all the cutting and chopping.

Bacon-Wrapped Stuffed Shrimp
with Corn Maque Choux

Serves 4

Way back when, this was a leftover dish made with Spam, corn chowder, and bacon. We'd whisk it up, make it nice and creamy, then we'd put fried shrimp on top.

½ cup butter, divided use
1 cup minced onions, reserve ½ for sauce
1 cup minced celery, reserve ½ for sauce
1 (8 ounce) can white crab meat, drained
3 tablespoons Best Foods mayonnaise
3/4 cup bread crumbs
14 pieces shrimp, peeled, deveined and butterflied
14 strips thinly sliced bacon
½ block butter
1 (15-ounce) can cream corn
1 cup heavy cream

Preheat oven to 375°F. In a medium sauté pan, add butter, ½ cup onions, and ½ cup celery. Sauté for 4 minutes. Fold in crab meat, mayonnaise, and bread crumbs (slowly) until you get a nice binding consistency. Let cool for 4 to 5 minutes. Once cooled, stuff shrimp with 1 teaspoon of crab mixture, wrap with a bacon strip, and place evenly in a baking pan. Bake for 10 to 15 minutes or until bacon is golden brown.

To make the *macque choux,* melt ½ block butter in a saucepan. Add remaining onions and celery and sauté for about 4 minutes. Add cream corn and cook for an additional 3 to 4 minutes. Add heavy cream and cook until for 3 minutes.

Spoon *macque choux* onto a flat dish and top with stuffed shrimp. Enjoy!

Garlic Shrimp Pasta

Serves 2

1 tablespoon olive oil
1 tablespoon crushed garlic
6 to 8 shrimp, cooked
6 to 8 grape tomatoes, halved
6 to 8 brussels sprouts, halved
1 to 2 servings of leftover spaghetti noodles, cooked
3 to 4 ounces brie cheese
1 to 1½ cups marinara sauce
1 tablespoon olive oil
2 tablespoons basil pesto
1 teaspoon Parmesan cheese
1 teaspoon chopped garlic

Heat olive oil in a thick sauté pan and add garlic; cook over medium-high heat for about 1 minute to season pan. Add shrimp, tomatoes and brussels sprouts just to heat up for a few minutes, then remove from pan and set aside. Because the shrimp is already cooked, you don't want to overcook it.

Reheat leftover noodles with brie in same pan until cheese melts and noodles separate, then add marinara sauce and pesto. Combine until heated and place on a serving platter.

Reheat shrimp, tomatoes, and brussels sprouts for one minute. Sprinkle with Parmesan cheese and mix. Pour on top of noodles and serve.

Brie cheese has a creamy texture and a unique but mild taste. In this recipe, it really allows the flavor of the garlic and the pesto to shine. Brussels sprouts have a strong, almost bitter flavor which gets balanced out by the sweetness of the grape tomatoes and marinara sauce.

Mung Beans with Chicharron and Shrimp

Serves 4

2 (14-ounce) packages split mung beans
2 tomatoes, diced
1 clove garlic, minced
1 red onion, diced
1 pound chicharron, sliced
1 (32-ounce) box chicken stock
1 package (21 to 25 pieces) shrimp, peeled and deveined
1½ cups bitter melon shoots
1½ cups malunggay leaves

In a large bowl, soak mung beans for 30 to 45 minutes.

In a skillet, sauté tomatoes, garlic, and red onions for 10 minutes. Add chicharron and cook for 15 minutes. Add mung beans and chicken stock and cook for 20 minutes. Add shrimp and cook for 2 minutes. Mix well. Lastly, add bitter melon shoots and malunggay leaves.

This hearty dish features mung beans simmered to perfection with succulent roast pork and juicy shrimp. The rich, savory flavors meld together beautifully. It may sound crazy, but sometimes I eat this with really nice chips like a dip because it's so rich and creamy.

CHEF DICKSON ALVARADO (PIER 9)

One of my favorite things to make is ceviche, which is dish of fish or shellfish marinated in citrus juices that cook the seafood. You go down to South America, Florida, the Caribbean, you'll find a variety of ceviches with different flavors. In Hawai'i, you can use locally caught mahimahi or ono. It's a quick and easy dish to make that tastes fresh, light, and has tons of flavor.

Shrimp Ceviche

Serves 4

1 pound raw medium shrimp, peeled and deveined
Juice of 1 lemon
Juice of 1 lime
4 calamansi, cut in half
¾ teaspoon salt
2 tablespoons olive oil
1 small red onion, sliced
½ teaspoon red pepper flakes
½ tablespoon chili pepper water
½ cup chopped tomatoes
½ cup chopped sweet red peppers
½ cup chopped yellow peppers
1 medium Asian pear, sliced and julienned
½ cup chopped cucumbers
1 small avocado, cut into cubes
⅓ cup fresh cilantro, finely chopped (reserve 1 tablespoon for garnish)

In a bowl, add shrimp, citrus juices, and salt. Marinate for 4 minutes. Add olive oil, onions, red pepper flakes, chili pepper water, tomatoes, peppers, Asian pear, and cucumbers. Fold in avocado and cilantro. Garnish with remaining cilantro.

Maui-Style Smoked Octopus with Lūʻau Leaves and Coconut Milk

Serves 4

2 pounds smoked octopus
½ cup butter
2 medium sweet Maui onions, diced
2 (13.5-ounce) cans coconut milk
1 pinch Hawaiian salt
1 teaspoon Maui sugar
3 pounds boiled lūʻau leaves

Slice smoked octopus into bite-size pieces and set aside.

In a skillet, melt butter and sauté onions until translucent (about 5 minutes). Add octopus and sauté for 2 minutes. Stir in coconut milk and salt. Add sugar and stir. Slowly add lūʻau leaves and mix well. Let simmer for 20 minutes until tender.

Squid lūʻau is made with lūʻau or taro leaves and coconut milk. In this recipe, we use smoked octopus. Lūʻau leaves come from the kalo or taro plant which is a staple in Hawaiian cooking. The leaves cannot be eaten raw and must be properly cooked. In this recipe, Marja already had boiled lūʻau leaves ready to cook with.

Scan to watch Sam
make this dish!

Vegan Tofu Hekka

Serves 4

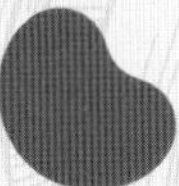

NATIONAL KIDNEY FOUNDATION®
of Hawaii

1 tablespoon oil
1 carrot, julienned
1 small onion, sliced
4 stalks celery, sliced diagonally
5 stalks asparagus, sliced diagonally
2 cloves garlic, minced
1 tablespoon chopped ginger
½ bunch watercress, chopped
3 tablespoons low sodium vegetable stock
1 block firm tofu, cubed
1 tablespoon honey
Mrs. Dash Seasoning, to taste

Heat oil in frying pan, add vegetables and stir-fry until tender. Add vegetable stock, tofu, and honey. Mix well. Season with Mrs. Dash to taste.

COREY AND LAUREEN SPENCER ‘OHANA

Did you know Julia Child loved tofu? We talked about that one time way back when. She saw how they made it and she just loved it. Tofu is so versatile and a great addition to any stir-fry. It soaks up the flavors of everything it’s cooked with—sauces, vegetables, whatever.

Tofu Stir-Fry
with Sweet Teriyaki Sauce

Serves 2 to 4

2 tablespoons olive oil
1 tablespoon minced garlic
1 tablespoon minced ginger
1 cup small broccoli florets
2 cups chopped bok choy
1 carrot, julienned
2 tablespoons sweet teriyaki sauce
8 ounces firm tofu, cubed
½ cup chopped onions
1 bell pepper, cored, seeded and julienned
6 to 8 asparagus spears, chopped
Salt, to taste

In a thick sauté pan, heat olive oil on medium. Add garlic, ginger, broccoli, bok choy, and carrots. Drizzle teriyaki sauce over vegetables and toss well. Turn up heat to medium-high. Add tofu and drizzle with more teriyaki sauce on top of the tofu. Toss and let simmer. Add onions, bell peppers, asparagus, and salt. Toss well and serve.

CHRIS, CLAIRE AND KA'IWA CHOY

Pesto Pizza and Margherita Pizza

Serves 2

2 naan bread
2 to 3 tablespoons pesto
½ cup shredded mozzarella cheese
8 leaves fresh basil, chiffonade, divided use
2 to 3 tablespoons marinara sauce
2 slices buffalo mozzarella cheese

Preheat oven to 400°F.

Place naan bread on a baking sheet. On one naan bread, evenly spread pesto sauce and mozzarella cheese. Garnish with half of the basil leaves. On the other naan bread, evenly spread marinara sauce and place buffalo mozzarella cheese on top. Garnish with remaining basil leaves. Bake for 8 to 10 minutes.

This is my granddaughter's recipe and it's a simple, perfect little recipe kids can make themselves as a snack or quick dinner. Claire uses naan bread which makes it quick and easy. There's also a lot of possible toppings your kids can use. And although there's a lot of great sauces out there you can buy at the store, you can also make your own sauce which is very easy.

CHRIS, CLAIRE AND KA'IWA CHOY

Cooking with my grandkids is always so fun. I love seeing what they create. For this dish, I was Ka'iwa's sous chef. You may have seen versions of this dish on social media, which is what inspired Ka'iwa to try this dish. There's a lot of cooking going on out there on social media, and the good thing about that is it's inspiring young people to try different dishes in the kitchen. They'll learn what works, what doesn't, and it will make them better and more confident chefs.

Feta Pasta

Serves 4

2½ cups cherry tomatoes
1 block feta cheese
3 cloves garlic, chopped
1 teaspoon garlic salt
½ teaspoon black pepper
2 tablespoons olive oil
8 leaves fresh basil, chiffonade
4 leaves fresh basil, whole for garnish
½ box farfalle (bow-tie) pasta, cooked

Preheat oven to 375°F.

In a casserole dish, add tomatoes, feta cheese, garlic, garlic salt, pepper, and olive oil. Top with basil (chiffonade). Bake for 10 minutes. Add cooked pasta and mix well. Garnish with whole leaf basil and cherry tomatoes.

DESSERTS AND DRINKS

Banana Lumpia with Jackfruit

Serves 4 to 6

6 ripe apple bananas
1 (12-ounce jar) jackfruit, sliced into strips
12 lumpia wrappers
1 cup brown sugar
1½ cups cooking oil

Peel bananas and slice in half lengthwise. Place a banana slice and slices of jackfruit in one corner of a lumpia wrapper. Sprinkle banana and jackfruit with brown sugar and roll in the wrapper, tucking in the ends. Use water (or egg whites) to seal the wrapper.

In a skillet, heat the oil over medium heat. Fry each banana lumpia until crispy and golden brown, approximately 3 to 4 minutes. Remove from heat and place on a plate with paper towels to absorb excess oil. Sprinkle with more brown sugar. Once the sugar caramelizes, serve warm and enjoy!

These crispy spring rolls are filled with sweet bananas and jackfruit, then fried to golden perfection. They're a sweet treat that's crunchy on the outside and deliciously soft on the inside. When frying them, the trick is to not use too much oil. The lumpia shouldn't be fully submerged—just about halfway.

LARRY AND DARIA MOORE

Doughnut Bread Pudding

Serves 4

6 doughnuts
2 eggs
1½ cups milk
1 tablespoon sugar
¼ teaspoon cinnamon
½ teaspoon vanilla extract
1 teaspoon butter

Preheat oven to 350°F.

Slice doughnuts into cubes and place in a small baking pan. In a bowl, add eggs, milk, sugar, cinnamon and vanilla extract. Mix well. Pour mixture over donuts. Bake for 45 minutes.

When done, place on a serving plate and spread butter on top.

Get creative with some leftover doughnuts, especially if they're day-old. Bread pudding is the perfect dish to make using any kind of stale bread you don't want to waste. A variety of doughnuts with or without frosting, sprinkles, whatever, will make a sweet, delicious bread pudding.

Peach Melba

Serves 2

1 (15-ounce) can peach halves with juice
1½ cups brown sugar
6 tablespoons butter
Juice from ½ lemon
½ teaspoon cinnamon
2 tablespoons rum
Vanilla ice cream

Drain peaches (reserve syrup) and set aside.

In a saucepan, heat brown sugar and butter. Add peach syrup. Once melted, add a squeeze of lemon. Stir well. Add peaches, cinnamon, and rum. Stir and cook until liquid becomes syrupy. Serve over ice cream and enjoy!

A melba is a version of a flambé. You heat up the peaches and make a nice syrup in the pan with the sugar and butter, and that goes right over a nice scoop of ice cream. I showed John how to make this for his wife to celebrate Valentine's Day.

This is a delicious, easy-to-make dessert that looks like you spent a lot of time on it, but it's just a matter of prepping the fruit and assembling everything. You can sprinkle the tops of the finished pastries with powdered sugar to give them that holiday feel.

Mixed Berry Tart

Serves 4 to 6

1 box Peppermill Puff Pastry Sheets
1 box sugar-free vanilla pudding
1 carton blueberries
1 carton raspberries
1 carton strawberries, sliced
1 tablespoon lemon juice
Honey
1 (8-ounce) container Sugar-Free Cool Whip

Bake puff pastry and pudding as directed.

In a medium bowl, mix berries and lemon juice. Slightly macerate the berries. Add drizzle of honey and set aside.

Once puff pastry is cooled, cut in half lengthwise, remove top layer and set aside. Spoon pudding in an even layer on the puff pastry. Add layer of berries and a dollop of Cool Whip. Cover with the top layer of puff pastry.

Sam's Pumpkin Crunch

Serves 15 to 20

All great holiday meals have to have a smattering of desserts. But there's always one you want to serve first and foremost. This is the most googled dessert when you search for Sam Choy desserts. But you know, I gotta be honest. I didn't create this recipe. I did it one time in one of my many cooking classes and somebody took that recipe, put it out there and boy, it's been really big. Pumpkin Crunch is a really popular dessert in Hawai'i. A lot of people make it.

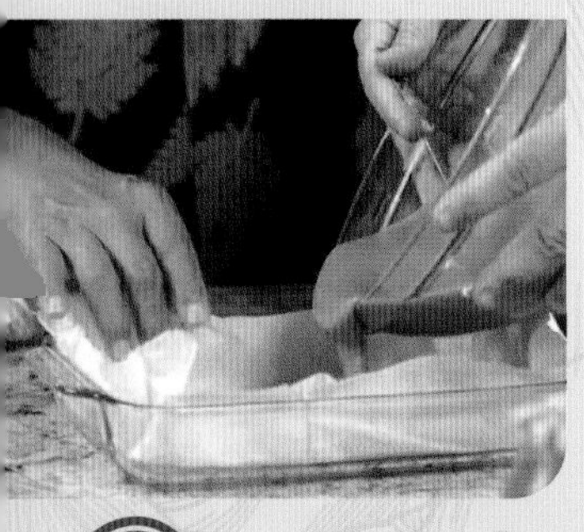

1 (13-ounce) can pumpkin
1 (12-ounce) can evaporated milk
1 cup sugar
3 eggs
1 teaspoon cinnamon
1 box yellow cake mix
1 cup chopped nuts
1 cup melted butter
Whipped cream

Preheat oven to 350°F.

Mix pumpkin, evaporated milk, sugar, and eggs and pour into greased, parchment-lined 9x13-inch cake pan. Spread half of the yellow cake mix (dry) over batter, sprinkle with nuts and remaining cake mix. Pour melted butter evenly over top. Bake for 50 minutes.

When cool, loosen pumpkin crunch from side of pan with a knife. Invert pan onto platter (the top becomes the crust). Top with whipped cream.

Johnny's Midnight Delight

Serves 1

1 whole banana, peeled
2 ounces Screwball Peanut Butter Whiskey
2 scoops Kona Coffee Ice Cream
1 ounce heavy cream

Combine all ingredients in a blender and blend until smooth.

Ashley Hupp created this peanut butter and banana drink for John Veneri. It's like a smoothie for those over twenty-one.

Uncle Sam's Mango Hard Lemonade

Social influencer Ashley Hupp knows that I love mango, so she created this hard lemonade just for me. It's a batch cocktail meaning there's a lot of liquor, so it's meant to share with lots of friends. It's perfect for a party, or keep it in your fridge and enjoy it when friends come over. Serving it over ice dilutes it so it isn't too potent.

1 bottle Hapa Hawaiian Vodka
½ bottle Triple Sec
Homemade mango simple syrup (1 cup each mango, sugar, and water combined and boiled)
32 ounces pineapple juice
2½ quarts fresh lemonade

Combine all ingredients; stir. Serve over ice.

GLOSSARY

'Ahi—Hawaiian name for yellowfin or bigeye tuna. When the term 'ahi is used, it is assumed that it is fresh tuna, not canned. Served in the Islands as sashimi (Japanese-style raw fish) with a spicy mustard-soy sauce dip. Also the fish of choice in poke. 'Ahi keeps well when salted and dried. Substitute fresh blackfin or bluefin tuna.

'Āweoweo—Hawaiian name given to various red fishes from the Bigeye family. Delicious fried whole in hot vegetable oil and eaten patiently with chopsticks to remove all sharp bones.

Bitter melon shoots—Edible greens that can be eaten from the bitter melon plant, a tropical vine related to zucchini, squash, pumpkin, and cucumber. Bitter melon is often used as a vegetable and is a staple in many Asian cuisines.

Bok choy—Chinese word for a type of cabbage with dark green leaves and long white stems. Also known as *pak choy* or Chinese white cabbage.

Burrata—A semi-soft, fresh cheese that originated in Southern Italy. It has a firm outer layer and a creamy, spreadable center made from fresh mozzarella and stracciatella, a mixture of cream and shredded mozzarella.

Calamanci, calamansi, calamondin—Refers to the low-acid Filipino lemon, about the size of a large olive.

Char siu—Chinese word for Cantonese-style marinated pork that is barbecued or roasted. It has a red color and a sweet and spicy flavor.

Chayote, sayote—A plant native to Central America, this prolific vine produces 1 to 2 pounds of squash-like fruits. The shoots of the vine can also be eaten. Locally, it is known as pipinola.

Chinese five-spice powder—A fragrant, spicy, and slightly sweet spice mixture made from ground star anise, Szechuan peppercorns, fennel seeds, cloves, and cinnamon.

Choi sum—Chinese word for a green leafy type of cabbage with tender, mildly flavored leaves. Often stir-fried with garlic and oyster sauce.

Chojang sauce—Or *chogochujang,* is a Korean dipping sauce made from the traditional chili paste gochujang. Chojang is made by adding vinegar and other seasonings to gochujang, such as sugar and sesame seeds. The result is a spicy-sweet sauce that's often used in mixed rice dishes like bibimbap or as a vinaigrette for dipping raw vegetables or seafood.

Chow fun—Chinese word for stir-fried, flat rice noodles.

Chow mein noodles—Chinese word for soft-fried wheat or egg noodles; sold dried or fresh.

Daikon—Japanese word for a large Asian radish, usually white in color, used in

Japan and Korea for soups and pickles or shredded raw for salads and garnishes. Flavors range from mild to spicy-hot. Available fresh, pickled, or preserved. Substitute turnips or radishes.

Enoki mushrooms—A type of cooking mushroom often used in Asian cooking; has long, slender, white stems, with tiny caps and a mild, delicate flavor.

Fishcake—Fish cakes are made from minced or ground fish or other seafood, mixed with a starchy ingredient, and then fried or steamed. They can be eaten as a snack or appetizer, or used in soups, stews, and boxed lunches.

Gochugaru—A very spicy, coarsely ground Korean chili powder similar to crushed red pepper flakes in texture, traditionally made from sun-dried peppers without the seeds.

Hawaiian chili pepper—A very small (1/2- to 1-inch long) and extremely hot chili pepper grown in Hawai'i. It ranks about nine out of ten on the hotness scale. Substitute Thai bird chilies or any small hot chili pepper.

Jack fruit—Large, oblong fruit with spiny skin. The starchy flesh tastes like a combination of apple, pineapple, mango, and banana. Used throughout Asian cuisines in both savory and sweet dishes. The seeds are edible and when roasted and taste like chestnuts.

Japanese pear—There are many varieties of this type of pear that are firm and crunchy when ripe. Most are delicately sweet in flavor and quite juicy. Also known as Asian pear.

Kabocha pumpkin—A Japanese variety of winter squash. It has a grayish-green thick skin with orange flesh that is very tender, smooth, and slightly sweet. Also known as Japanese pumpkin and *nankwa,* the Okinawan name for all pumpkins.

Kaffir lime leaves—Glossy, dark green leaves that have a floral-citrus aroma. Like bay leaves, kaffir leaves should be removed before serving to prevent family and guests from accidentally choking on stiff leaves. Substitute lemongrass or lime zest.

Kakuma shoots—A Japanese delicacy made from the young, unfurled shoots of the native Hawaiian tree fern, hāpu'u.

Kalbi—Korean word for barbecued short ribs that have been marinated in soy sauce, ginger, and sugar.

Kalo—Hawaiian word for taro, a kind of aroid cultivated for food. Taro has been a staple food in Hawai'i since ancient times. It is a perennial herb displaying a cluster of long-stemmed, heart-shaped leaves. All parts of the plant were eaten.

Kālua—Hawaiian method of cooking food in an underground pit called an imu. Usually refers to a whole pig cooked in an imu.

Kamaboko—Japanese word for red or white fish cakes made of puréed white fish mixed with potato starch and salt, then steamed. Used mostly in Japanese soup or noodle dishes.

Kimchi, kimchee—Korean word for a pickled vegetable dish usually made with Chinese cabbage (won bok), vinegar, salt, garlic, and chili peppers. Can be very hot and spicy. Substitute pickled cucumbers or cabbage with garlic and chili peppers.

Lap cheong (lup cheong, lop cheong or lop chong)—Chinese word for slender, aromatic, dried pork sausages. Has a dried texture similar to pepperoni and contains a lot of fat. Substitute Portuguese sausage. Also known as Chinese sausage.

Lemongrass—Citrus-scented grass with a distinctive lemon flavor and aroma. Its long, woody stalk resembles the white part of a green onion. Substitute kaffir lime leaves.

Liliko'i—Hawaiian passion fruit. Passion fruit is the sweet-sour, yellow, lemon-sized variety, while the purple-skinned liliko'i is sweeter. Substitute frozen concentrate liliko'i or orange juice.

Long bean—A green vegetable used widely in Asian cuisines. An ingredient in Filipino *pinacbet.*

Lū'au leaves—The young green tops of the taro root. Substitute fresh spinach.

Mahimahi—Dolphin fish; has a firm, pink flesh. Best fresh but often available frozen. A standard in Island restaurants and markets. Substitute snapper, catfish, or halibut.

Malunggay (marungay) leaves—Leaves with a citrus-like and slightly bitter flavor used in Filipino cuisine.

Miso—Japanese word for fermented paste of soy mixed with *koji* and salt. Rice miso uses rice as *koji,* and barley miso uses barley as *koji.* The length of the aging process creates the differences in the color of miso, such as red miso or white miso. There are varieties of miso, such as sweet miso, which uses more *koji,* and salty miso. Use according to your taste. Substitute condensed chicken broth blended with a small amount of tofu.

Mochiko—Japanese word for a form of flour made from sweet rice and used in various recipes in Hawai'i, including mochiko chicken, butter mochi, chichi dango, and white sauce. Also used in cooking and baking as a flour substitute for those who have gluten (protein contained in wheat seeds) allergies.

Moi—Hawaiian name for small threadfin fish. In old Hawai'i, only royalty were allowed to eat this fish. Sweet; best prepared steamed or baked whole.

Nori—Japanese word for a deep purple or greenish-black seaweed generally sold dried, in tissue-thin 8-inch sheets; frequently used in Japanese cooking, often for wrapping sushi.

Ogo—Japanese name for a reddish-brown seaweed. Several Hawai'i aquaculture operations grow ogo, and it is widely available. Boil quickly, and after the color turns bright green, cool and use it for salads and sunomono (vinegar dishes). Ogo is often used for poke in Hawaiʻi. Substitute finely julienned crisp cucumbers plus bits of dried nori seaweed, or try rinsed sweet or dill pickles.

Okinawan sweet potato—Purple sweet potato. It is rich in antioxidants, which help prevent cardiovascular disease and cancer.

Ono—Hawaiian name for a large mackerel. Flesh has a white flaky texture. Substitute mahimahi, halibut, cod, kingfish, swordfish, monkfish, or orange roughy. Known as wahoo.

Oyster sauce—A concentrated dark brown sauce made from oysters, brine, and shoyu. Used in many stir-fried dishes to impart a full, rich flavor. Substitute regular or vegetarian forms.

Panko—Japanese word for crispy, large-flaked bread crumbs that add more texture than ordinary bread crumbs. Substitute fine dry breadcrumbs.

Pāpio—Hawaiian name for young or small white ulua. Great fried whole in hot oil. Also known as giant jack trevally.

Patis—Filipino word for a pungent fish sauce made from salted, fermented fish.

Poi—Hawaiian staple; made from steamed taro that is pounded to a paste with the addition of water until it reaches a consistency that can be consumed by scooping with one, two, or three fingers.

Poke—Hawaiian word meaning to slice or to cut into small bite-sized pieces; now refers to a traditional Hawaiian dish made of sliced raw fish, Hawaiian salt, seaweed, and chilies. It can be purchased ready-made in most grocery stores today.

Portuguese sausage—Spicy pork sausage seasoned with onions, garlic, and pepper. Can be mild or hot. Substitute Italian sausage.

Quinoa—Small grain from Central America that is used much like couscous or rice. Considered a superfood high in protein and vitamin E, and low in calories.

Sashimi—A Japanese dish of very thin slices of fresh, raw fish. Usually served with a hot mustard and soy sauce with thin-sliced ginger on the side.

Sesame oil—A dense, flavorful oil pressed from sesame seeds. When untoasted seeds are cold-pressed, a very clear and mild-flavored oil is extracted. Toasted sesame seeds produce a dark brown and strong-flavored oil.

Shiitake mushroom—A medium to large umbrella-shaped mushroom. It has floppy tan to dark brown caps with edges that tend to roll under. Shiitakes have a woodsy, smoky flavor. Can be purchased fresh or dried in Asian groceries. Also called black Chinese mushrooms and forest mushrooms.

Shirataki—Japanese word for gelatinous, noodle-like strips made from tuberous root flour.

Soba noodles—Japanese word for buckwheat noodles, thin and light brown in color, and eaten warm or cold. Substitute angel hair pasta.

Somen—Japanese word for very thin, white noodles made of wheat flour. Usually served cold with a light-flavored dipping broth. Substitute vermicelli.

Soy sauce—Salty liquid made from fermented boiled soybeans, roasted barley or wheat, MSG, and salt. Dark soy sauce is stronger than light soy sauce. Also called shoyu.

Spam—Hormel's canned meat; popular in Hawai'i, especially in making musubi.

Sriracha hot sauce—American-made Vietnamese hot sauce made from sun-ripened chili peppers, vinegar, garlic, sugar, and salt. Similar to the hot sauces of Vietnam and Thailand.

Taegu—Korean word for a popular appetizer made from shredded cuttlefish or codfish seasoned in a spicy sauce. Served with salads, noodle dishes, or as a garnish.

Ti leaves—Leaves of the ti plant used to steam and bake fish and vegetables. Often called "Hawaiian aluminum foil." The leaves are not consumed. Available at wholesale floral shops. Substitute banana leaves, grape leaves, or corn husks.

Tobiko—Japanese name for flying fish roe. Usually more expensive than masago roe. Used in sushi for crunch and orange color. Substitute any fish roe.

Tofu—Japanese word for a bland-flavored soybean curd that can be custard-like in texture (soft tofu) or quite firm. The firm and extra-firm forms are generally used in stir-frying or deep-frying.

Ube—Filipino word for purple yam, often used in a variety of desserts.

'Ulu—Hawaiian word for breadfruit. A bland, starchy vegetable widely used in the Pacific Islands but difficult to get on the U.S. mainland. Breadfruit trees were brought to Hawai'i from Tahiti. Fruit can weigh over 10 pounds and has a warty rind. Turns yellow-green when mature and is sweet when ripe. Substitute baking potatoes.

Unagi—Japanese name for fresh-water eel. Most commonly eaten on top of hot rice and called unagi-donburi.

Wasabi—Japanese horseradish; a pungent root with an extremely strong, sharp flavor that comes in both powder and paste forms. Pale green in color and produces a sharp, tingling sensation on the palate. Substitute hot dry mustard.

Watercress—Member of the mustard family with crisp, dark green leaves that have a slightly bitter and peppery taste.

Winter melon—Ash gourd, is a mild-tasting fruit that's often used as a vegetable in Asian cuisines in soups, sweets, and beverages.

Yakisoba—Japanese word for wok-fried thick soba noodles.

INDEX

A

B

C

E

F

G

H

J

K

Q

S

T

U

V

W

Z